PROJECT DAD

MAKE EVERY DAY AN ADVENTURE WITH DAD!

PROJECT DAD

MAKE EVERY DAY AN ADVENTURE WITH DAD!

Bath · New York · Singapore · Hong Kong · Cologne · Delhi
Melbourne · Amsterdam · Johannesburg · Shenzhen

This edition published by Parragon Books Ltd in 2015

Parragon Books Ltd
Chartist House
15–17 Trim Street
Bath BA1 1HA, UK
www.parragon.com

Written by Lee Coan and Diane Ashmore
Illustrated by Dynamo
Designed by Lexi L'Esteve and Rhys Prosser
Project photos by Henry Sparrow
Project managed and edited by Cheryl Warner

Text on how to build a shelter and how to build a campfire has been provided by Paul Weller of
Keswick Canoe and Bushcraft
Monster Truck on page 106 is modelled by Harry Voss

ISBN 978-1-4723-8077-7
Printed in China

Contents

Contents

INTRODUCTION

Imagine being able to drive your own Monster Truck, be a knight or princess in your very own castle or be able to check some bugs into your own bug hotel. This book brings your child's imagination to life with 20 projects that any daring Dad can make with or for a child. From being a great explorer, camping out in the wilds of your own backyard to making a puppy pom-pom, there's a variety of activities to choose from to please any child.

The only predictable thing about the weather is that it is unpredictable, so activities for rainy days are as valuable as those for discovering the great outdoors. This book contains two sections, one to cover outdoor activities and the other to usefully cover activities for around the home. Not that home-based activities are any less adventurous — making a target and catapult is just as fun and exciting as going on a scavenger hunt. Once you've made the target and catapult, there are endless games to play as you get better at hitting the target.

The crafts and activities in this book are designed for Dad to make and involve a child where he thinks appropriate. For example, Dad can do all of the cutting and gluing for the castle project and involve his little helper in decorating and painting the castle. For the shadow puppet theatre, Dad could cut out the shapes and help glue them together, but the design of the puppets, the gripping storyline and the star performance is entirely the child's. Playing in the castle or creating a shadow puppet play will make the time fly by. The idea is to work as an A-team, creating imaginative projects that can make great life-size toys for hours of fun afterwards.

Discovering the great outdoors is made into a big adventure with advice on creating a campfire, camping out in the wilds of your own garden, or becoming the next intrepid explorer with your own special kit. Exciting worlds can unfurl with the aid of seemingly mundane objects. With an explorer kit, you and your child can go on wild adventures with just an old suitcase, a magnifying glass, an old map and a dash of imagination. Camping out can incorporate a whole host of activities, including outdoor games, talking on tin-can telephones or stargazing. You could even create the outdoor shelter instead of using a tent for a whole day of outdoor activity.

Discovering the outdoors needn't be confined to your own backyard. The beach can become a magical place if you spend the day beachcombing, rock pooling or building a sandy version of a snowman — made from sand (obviously), with seaweed for hair and a pebble for the nose. You could even take the children on a scavenger hunt, giving them a list of items to find or they could make a nature scrapbook to record their discoveries.

Not all activities need a long list of tools to make them. The Imaginative Questions activity merely involves writing your questions on paper, wrapping them into swirls and inserting them in a jar to be unfurled at any time to spark up a conversation. To give your child a boost of confidence, get them to create an 'I Am Great' self-portrait. They can even make it as part of a time capsule to be uncovered years later. Whatever you or your child's interests may be, there is something in this book for everyone.

GET CRAFTING!

Craft activities don't have to be expensive or time-consuming. You can collect household items, such as cardboard boxes, drinks cartons, cereal boxes and even the tubes of kitchen or toilet rolls to use in your projects. It needn't cost a lot and it's also a great lesson on how to reuse items that are destined for the refuse site — transforming them with a bit of imagination into great play activities.

 The 'Dad Only' symbol used in the projects helps give guidance on what needs to be done by an adult. The idea is that you make the projects with your child, deciding when it is safe to involve them. The 'Dad Only' symbol usually highlights activities including cutting, sticking with a hot glue gun and anything that may involve sharp edges or hot materials. Children can help to draw out shapes or stick things together with double-sided sticky tape or craft glue instead. They will also have lots of fun using their creativity to decorate the projects.

Each project includes a list of items that you'll need. Most of them are items that you'll have around the home, but the list also includes the tools that you will need to make the project.

Some of the craft projects involve the use of a glue gun, which, although fun to use, should only be used by an adult because the glue gets very hot. Glue guns, available from craft suppliers, are great for ensuring a quick-drying, secure fixing for many types of materials. Solid glue sticks are inserted into the tool, which heats the glue and transforms it from a solid to a liquid. In its hot liquid state, the glue needs handling with care. The glue cools quickly and as it dries becomes solid again, giving a secure hold.

PVA or craft glue takes much longer to dry, and surfaces will sometimes need holding in place while it dries. Children can safely use craft glue and there are brands that are designed to wash out more easily from clothes. Another option is to use double-sided sticky tape, which is great for attaching paper or card surfaces that are not too heavy. Just stick to one of the surfaces, remove the film of paper on top and then attach the other surface.

In many of the projects, you'll also need to use a craft knife or scissors, which again should only be used by an adult. When cutting with a craft knife, it is a good idea to protect your work surface either with a cutting mat or, if you don't have one of those, a piece of thick cardboard (anything thick enough to protect the surface from cutting will suffice). Alternatively, you could use a workbench that you don't mind getting scratched on the surface or splashed with paint.

When using craft glue or paint, getting your child to wear old clothes or some kind of apron or overall is a great idea. Then there is no need to worry about ruining any clothes. Protecting surfaces with old newspapers or thick cardboard, if needed, means that you and your child can enjoy making the projects without worrying about ruining furniture.

The idea is to have fun making the craft projects safely and then have hours of fun with the finished results. Once you've mastered the basic designs, there are many ways to personalize these projects with pens, crayons or paints. You could even try collaging onto some of the projects, such as the Monster Truck, using pictures cut out from magazines and craft glue. The possibilities are endless!

ACTIVITIES FOR THE GREAT OUTDOORS

You can't beat getting out of the house to go on adventures, finding worlds waiting to be discovered. In this book, there are various activities to spark your child's imagination and while away the hours outside. You don't even have to go that far — adventures lie right on the doorstep, in your own garden, or you could just visit the nearest park.

There are many types of habitat that you can use or make to attract wildlife to your garden, from nest boxes, bird baths, and hedgehog houses to the simple and easy-to-make bug hotel described on page 18. A homemade bug hotel is guaranteed to check in some interesting creepy-crawlies. All you need is a flowerpot and a few bug-friendly materials.

Camping out needn't be in a faraway place in the middle of nowhere. You can pitch a tent or make a shelter in your own garden (see page 38). This is a great opportunity for stargazing and a chance to identify the important constellations. You don't need a fancy telescope to do this: there's a lot to see just with the naked eye. It could ignite a fascination for space in your child that lasts for years to come.

The best part about camping is the games and activities surrounding it. If you can't decide which games to play first, create an 'Activity Jar'. Everyone gets to write down their favourite games on pieces of paper, fold them up and place them in a jar. Then take it in turns picking from the jar to see what you get to play.

Creating a nature scrapbook or your own explorer kit (see pages 46 and 34) is a great way of initiating various games or activities. With your explorer kit ready, you could try playing 'I Spy', describing animals or plants you come across as you roam and getting others to guess the name. Or if there are enough people to take part, you could create two teams, each team scoring points for finding items on a list. The winners are the ones who spot everything first.

Making a nature scrapbook (see page 46) can spark an interest in art as well as nature. With just a few crayons and a piece of paper, you could take rubbings of different types of bark, for example, sticking them in the scrapbook as you go along. With just a pencil, or a few coloured pencils, you could draw whatever catches the eye as you take a walk. Write up a brief description, the time and the place to record what you've found.

Making a glider (see page 30) or a kite (see page 50) is just the beginning of an adventure. After decorating them with your favourite colours, it's time to visit the park. You could make two or more kites or gliders and have races with them. Remember to fly your glider or kite on a day with a gentle breeze for the best results, allowing it to fly further and stay in one piece.

Holidays can be a great time to play outdoor games. A visit to the beach provides plenty of scope for activities involving all the family. As well as making the sandman, mentioned on page 58, you could collect pebbles and make them into pictures in the sand. Or build a car in the sand, large enough to sit in. Try making a dam or even a channel to be filled up by water as it crashes on the beach.

ACTIVITIES FOR AROUND THE HOME

A day around the home doesn't have to mean a dull day. This section of the book will arm you with a range of activities and craft projects to keep your child occupied for hours. You don't need to have lots of fancy toys or equipment as just a simple afternoon of baking can provide hours of fun for your child.

The crafts and activities in this book are mainly designed for Dad to make, using the 'Dad Only' symbol as a guide and involving a child where you think appropriate. Dad will do most of the cutting and gluing with the glue gun, but children will love decorating the projects and can personalize them to their heart's content. Use water-based craft paints, which are easy to wash away and non-toxic, or thick felt-tip pens or crayons.

The Crusher-bot Puppet (see page 80) offers a great opportunity for imaginative decoration. Paint his teeth white and add eyelashes to his table-tennis-ball eyes. You could use silver water-based paint or glue and cover him with kitchen foil to give him a robotic metallic finish.

The Monster Truck (see page 106) would look fantastic painted racing red or covered with squares of tissue paper or pictures cut from a magazine. You could also paint a layer of PVA glue on top to give it a sheen.

Let your child be the king or queen of the castle with the project on page 62. They can decorate it with coloured pens or pencils or glue pictures of knights or princesses onto the sides. It needn't end there — get them to dress up as a little princess or prince.

Making a shadow puppet theatre is more than just a craft project. Once you've made the theatre (see page 100) and the screen to capture the shadow, it's time to create the puppets and a story to tell. You don't just have to stick to a simple black silhouette; you could use a doll, a twig, your hand and fingers or anything that has an interesting shape. Why not use the sock caterpillar (see page 112) as a shadow puppet? You can use a table lamp as a light source or a torch that can be moved to change the shape of the shadow.

Let your imagination run wild when it comes to the story or try a simple fairytale. One person can move the puppets, another could read out the story and, of course, you need to invite other members of the family or friends to an exclusive performance as the audience.

Once you've made the catapult and target (see page 72), screw up some balls of old newspaper and get practising. When you've got the hang of it, have a game of who can hit the target the most number of times, increasing the challenge by moving the target further and further away.

Activities to do at home can be as simple as drawing with crayons. You could pencil in some shapes for them to colour or get them to draw their own designs. If they are not keen on drawing, finger painting is also a great option. Just make sure to cover all surfaces and get them to wear old clothes. A great game is to draw a character's head on a piece of paper and fold it over so the next person can only see the bottom of the head. Then that person draws the arms and the next draws a body and legs. The results can be hilarious!

THE GREAT OUTDOORS

Explore the world outside with these **10** fun activities!

Build Your Own Bug Hotel

Make a simple bug hotel for attracting and observing creepy-crawlies.

Children have a strange fascination with creepy-crawlies. If it's slimy, hairy and ugly, with wiggly antennae, 88 legs and 13 boggly eyes, chances are they'll want it as a pet. Creating a bug hotel is a great way for your child to get hands-on with insects, whilst also giving the nature in your garden a helping hand to survive. It really couldn't be easier or cheaper to create a bug hotel. You can use all kinds of scraps (see the 'You will need' section below) — any natural plant life that's lying around your garden is fantastic for creating the equivalent of a five-star hotel. Insects, such as beetles, spiders, ladybirds and bumblebees, will love it. So get creative and don't limit yourself to our suggestions — some people even stuff bits of old bricks and their old smelly socks in their bug hotels! Get as creative as you want, every bug hotel is unique.

You will need:
- old flowerpot (or more if you like)
- a selection of bug-friendly materials, such as garden trimmings, grass cuttings, compost, bamboo, dead wood, hay, straw, leaves, sticks, bark, cones, stones, parts of brick and old tiles
- magnifying glass
- wood pallets or logs (optional)
- bricks (optional)

DAD TIP

Use a well-hidden video camera or webcam to spy on bug activity when you're not around, so you can keep an eye on your hotel's guests.

GETTING STARTED

Work with your child to create your own custom-made bug hotel. Turn your flowerpot on its side, so the bugs will be able to crawl in and out easily. Start stuffing your bits and pieces inside the pot, keeping the heavy things towards the back and filling in the gaps with lighter items, such as straw or dead leaves. 'Snug as a bug' is not just a clever saying, insects genuinely do like cramped spaces, so make sure you squash as much as possible in there. Sections of old bamboo garden canes make a great resting spot for bees, whilst plant trimmings and grass cuttings make great nests for hibernating bugs. Spiders, centipedes and ladybirds love bark chippings, whilst bigger insects, such as beetles and woodlice, will be attracted to twigs. Try to find dry leaves to stuff in there too if possible, as these mimic the forest floor and will bring in a host of bugs looking for a cosy place to rest. You can never squash enough in your flowerpot, so really go for it. It's good to use things from your local environment as this will attract bugs from that same environment.

BRING ON THE BUGS

To make sure your bug hotel gets a lot of reservations from creepy-crawly holidaymakers, you need to find the right location for your completed hotel. Most insects do not like wind, so try to find a sheltered spot for your bug hotel flowerpot. Although many of the bugs might like it damp, you don't want a totally soggy hotel or the insides of your flowerpot might wash away, so try to find a spot in your garden that isn't going to get too wet should it rain.

Direct sunlight is not ideal as many creatures, such as earwigs and woodlice, will find this unbearable and chances are you won't have any guests other than bees (who love the sunshine). However, get the right spot and you will be amazed how quickly your bug hotel fills up. There are insects hidden everywhere out there and, within a couple of hours, we are sure you will have guests checking into your hotel. Carefully observe them using your magnifying glass and, if business is slow, you could always leave a little piece of rotting fruit at the front of your pot to drive the holidaymakers absolutely wild! You should expect to attract a whole range of bugs — bees, butterflies, wasps, insects, woodlice, spiders, ladybirds, slugs, snails — and even maybe some amphibians, such as frogs.

CREATE A BUG MANSION

If you've got space in your garden, you could build a larger, more elaborate version of a bug hotel. Use wood pallets or logs to build layers or floors of the hotel, with bricks placed between layers for support. Leave small spaces between the wood panels to stuff with the natural materials to attract the bugs and drill holes in the logs to allow insects to crawl in. If you place different types of material in the various spaces, you will attract different bugs to different 'rooms'. Ensure that the construction is well supported and weighted down with sufficient stones and bricks to make sure it survives all winds and weathers.

DAD TIP

If you don't have a plant pot, an old shoebox works just as well.

DAD TIP

Spring is the best time for getting a super-busy bug hotel, but you can attract bugs at any time of the year.

Build Your Own Natural Shelter

Make a natural shelter in the middle of the great outdoors.

Dens! There is perhaps no better way to while away the hours outdoors than by building a good old-fashioned den. Your child will love playing in their own space that you've created together.

You can build one almost anywhere — from deep within your local forest to under a small gathering of trees at your local park. All you need to do is master how to make an A-frame out of wood and then you're away. Once you've built your shelter, you and your child can use it to play in, to observe local wildlife from, or even to camp in if you're feeling extremely brave and adventurous (see page 38). Just always remember to dismantle your shelter and scatter any natural materials back where you found them, as they will become important habitat for local insects and wildlife.

This project shows you how to build a simple, single A-frame shelter, but you can make your den as large or as small as you like. If you require something bigger, just use multiple shorter poles and then line them up along the length of the longer pole.

You will need:

- long branch or pole (slightly longer than you are tall)
- two shorter poles (around half your height)
- branches and twigs of varying lengths
- leaves and forest debris
- rope
- knife
- waterproof tarpaulin or cover (optional)

DAD TIP

Don't use branches or logs any thicker than your wrist to cover your frame, as they may be too heavy for the frame to support.

GETTING STARTED

First of all, you need to choose your site. If you get the right location, with all the materials close by, then building your shelter will be much simpler and quicker to construct. You could be warm and dry or maybe ready to use your shelter in under an hour! So, look out for an area that has lots of fallen branches and leaf litter. Find an area of flat ground without too many lumps and bumps as this will be more comfortable to sleep on. Remember to check for any insect nests, such as ants' nests, before you start building and check you aren't building over any burrows. Have a look above you to see if you are underneath any hanging or dead branches that could fall onto your shelter. Finally, stay out of any hollows or holes as these will become puddles when it rains!

If you don't want to be too far away from home, you can also build an outdoor shelter in your own garden. You might need to go to a local park or woodland to source the materials before creating your shelter as you're not likely to have everything as readily available in your own garden.

THE BUILD

Once you've found the ideal spot to place your shelter, you can start to build.

1) Look for your fallen poles or branches — if you can find ones that have natural bends at the ends that will hook together and keep the frame more rigid, that's brilliant.

2) Make the shape of an upside-down 'V' with your two shorter poles. Securely tie the poles together at the top end where they cross over.

3) Now place one end of the longer pole across the join of the two shorter poles. Prop the other end of the longer pole on the ground so that the structure is balanced and steady. Securely tie the longer pole to the upside-down 'V' poles so that all three poles are tied together. The two shorter poles should be upright, with the longer pole as a prop to steady it.

4) If you want a larger or more substantial shelter, you can tie more upside-down 'V'-shaped poles along the whole length of the longer pole rather than resting the longer pole on the ground. This will create a steadier and larger structure.

5) Next, fill the space between the ground and the long pole with lots of branches and sticks. Use larger branches that you can trim to exactly fit the space at first and then fill in any gaps with smaller twigs. Make sure the branches and twigs don't stick up above the long pole if you want your shelter to be waterproof.

6) Then gather up handfuls of leaves and forest debris and use this to cover the frame. Start by covering the bottom of the shelter all the way around and then keep going from the bottom up to the longer pole. You will then need about a 10-cm/4-inch deep covering if you want to keep the rain out.

7) If you are camping and want a guaranteed waterproof shelter, you can place a light tarpaulin or waterproof covering over the frame as well, for added peace of mind.

DAD TIP

Never use mosses, ferns or wild flowers to cover your shelter as they may be very rare or even a protected species!

DAD TIP

Never break branches from a living tree, as this could let infection in and possibly even kill the tree.

How To Build A Campfire

Making a campfire can be such great fun if done properly and safely.

⚠ Health and safety alert! Take great care with this activity — fires need to be prepared and tended extremely carefully. Children need to be monitored at all times and kept at a safe distance from the fire. However, once you've got your 'Safety Dad' mode on, get really stuck in because campfires are such huge fun. Sitting by a campfire is a truly satisfying and rewarding experience and showing your child how to prepare and light it only adds to the enjoyment.

First of all, before you start you need to check the local laws in your area. If you are lighting a fire outside of your own property you need to check if you are legally allowed to do so. In England and Wales, for example, you must have the landowner's permission to light a fire (right to roam laws do not include allowing you to light fires). Even common land is usually owned by someone so plan ahead and check thoroughly beforehand. The law can vary — not just in every country, but also there can be local byelaws that may prohibit the lighting of fires in certain places. If you are going camping and were hoping to have a campfire, check online as there are websites that tell you which campsites allow fires. So check first, then get going…

You will need:

- spade
- stones
- bucket of water or fire extinguisher
- tinder, kindling and dry fuel wood (see the 'Gather your Equipment' section)
- lighter or matches

PREPARING THE SITE

Preparation is key. Taking several attempts or lighting your fire only to watch it smoulder and die out is a frustrating and demoralizing activity. So think carefully about where to site your fire. If you are camping, always set it up downwind of where you want to sit or pitch your tent. Choose a large open area so that you can move freely around your campfire, and keep well away from overhanging branches, grassland or peaty soil. Stony ground is perfect! Clear away any loose gravel, leaf debris or pine needles and remove any turf with your hands or a spade. Your cleared area should be at least twice the size of your planned fire — this also creates the 'no-go' area around the fire.

SAFETY FIRST

⚠ While you are lighting the fire, you need to keep your child away from the area and outside the 'no-go' area. You should place a ring of stones around the 'no-go' area so it is clear how close your child can get. Either get another adult to entertain your child or keep your child at a safe distance to observe what's going on, but with strict instructions not to come within the 'no-go' area.

Do not create a campfire in extremely windy conditions and do not build your fire on an upward slope as fire can spread quickly uphill. Always keep a bucket of cold water or fire extinguisher to hand so you can extinguish the fire quickly.

GATHER YOUR EQUIPMENT

If you construct your fire properly then it should light first time, every time. Gather your tinder, kindling and dry fuel wood — your child will enjoy hunting the local area with you and helping to gather suitable fuel. For tinder, you will need something that lights easily to start your fire with. This could be some birch or cherry tree bark, a ball of dry grass, screwed-up newspaper or even some cotton wool or sawdust. Next you'll need kindling — this should be twigs as thin as matchsticks, gathered into two fist-thick bundles.

You will also need some thicker sticks, about as thick as your thumb — these will be the fuel wood for your fire. You will also need a thick stick, about as thick as your wrist, to rest your kindling on. This will allow air to get into the fire.

BUILD IT UP

Lay down a flat bed of the fuel-wood sticks in the centre of your fire site. This will stop moisture from the ground turning to steam and putting your fire out. Place the thick stick at one end of the bed. Place the tinder on the bed of fuel-wood sticks about 5 cm/2 inches from the thick stick and…

⚠ LIGHT IT UP!

Once you've lit your tinder, take a bundle of your kindling and place it over the flame, resting one end of the bundle on the thick stick and the other end of the bundle on the bed of sticks. Do the same thing with a second bundle of kindling. In an ideal world, you need your two bundles to cross each other above the flame. When the kindling begins to crackle, add some more, and when it really takes, you can add the thicker fuel wood as you please.

⚠ KEEP THE FIRE BURNING

When the fire is burning, never leave it unattended and keep your child closely monitored and outside the 'no-go' area at all times. Keep your fire small, about as big as a football — do not allow it to grow into a bonfire. Make sure your child doesn't throw anything onto the fire.

PACKING UP

⚠ When you are ready to put out the fire, allow it to die out and ensure it is completely extinguished before leaving it unattended. Even once the flames have died out, the wood and ground will still be hot. Pour cold water over the fire and stir up the area with a large stick until you are sure everything has completely gone out.

DAD TIP

Gather the driest wood and kindling — look for twigs that are standing upright, close to the tree trunks, so they are sheltered from the rain.

Classic Glider

Have the best-looking glider in the park made from just a cereal box.

You will need:

- template from pages 122–123
- child-friendly scissors
- 1 x large cereal box
- scrap piece of corrugated card larger than the cereal box
- sticky tape
- craft knife (optional)
- ruler
- ball-point pen
- modelling clay
- paints and paintbrush, to decorate as you wish (optional)

Step 1:

Photocopy the templates on pages 122–123 or trace around them. Cut the templates into smaller sections with scissors.

Step 2:

Cut the cereal box along one of the seams and lay it out flat, with the printed side down, on top of a thick piece of corrugated card to protect the work surface. Use small lengths of sticky tape to secure the fuselage template onto the card, making sure the dotted centre line is over a crease.

⚠ Use either a craft knife or scissors to carefully cut out the fuselage, cutting along all the scissor lines. It's really important to be as accurate as possible when cutting out the glider as any mistakes could prevent your glider from flying properly.

Time to make: about 15 minutes

2.

Step 3:

Use small lengths of sticky tape to secure the wings template in place, avoiding any creases in the box.

 Carefully cut out the template along the scissor lines using a craft knife or scissors, protecting the work surface with the corrugated card.

Step 4:

Stick the tail template to the cardboard in the same way as the other parts. Using a ruler and a ball-point pen, press hard and draw along the solid lines to create a crease in the card. Don't press too hard to avoid tearing the card.

Step 5:

 Cut out the tail along the scissor lines.

Step 6:

Fold the fuselage in half with the printed side facing inwards. Gently slide the wings into the two forward-facing slots in the middle. Curl the wings slightly and slide it into the slots at the nose end.

Step 7:

Slide the tail into the slots at the back end of the fuselage until it can go no further.

Step 8:

Roll a marble-sized amount of modelling clay (or use the guide on the template) into a ball. Squash it between your fingers and thumb to about the size of the larger guide on the template.

Step 9:

Place the modelling clay disc into the nose and gently squeeze the sides of the glider together so the clay sticks to at least one side. Use a piece of sticky tape, about 4 cm/1½ inches long, to hold the two sides together. Decorate the glider with paints, if desired, especially underneath the wings and tail as this is what shows when it flies.

DAD TIP

Throw the glider gently to start with. If the glider climbs and then quickly falls (called a stall) you will need to add a little bit more modelling clay to the nose. Add a small amount at a time and test the glider until it flies without stalling. If the glider nose dives into the ground, remove a small bit of modelling clay from the nose and test until it flies a good distance before landing smoothly. To make your glider do a loop, gently bend the ailerons (movable flaps) on the tail upwards. The more you bend, the tighter the loop. Fly your glider on a calm day with only the gentlest of breezes otherwise it will not fly properly and could be blown away and damaged. Throwing your glider into a gentle breeze will give the best results. It will fly further and loop better. Do not attempt to fly on a rainy day.

Make Your Own Explorer Kit

Take a boring old suitcase or briefcase and turn it into an adventurer's toolkit, ready for any expedition.

You will need:

A small suitcase, briefcase, large lunchbox or an empty toolkit with a handle, as well as equipment for your kit (see right).

A child's imagination only needs a little kick-start and it can create whole worlds out of next to nothing. A saucepan on the head is an astronaut's hat, a stick is a cowboy's gun and a cardboard box is a knight's castle!

As a Dad, your child will happily take you on an adventure through their imagination with them — and making an explorer's kit can be a great first step into exploring that imagination together. By taking an old briefcase or suitcase and filling it with a few basic items, you can create something that will really get the imaginative juices flowing. It shouldn't take more than 15 minutes to create and it should be really inexpensive to make. Once you've got your kit, you and your child can go on wild adventures together. How about climbing the great mountain range that is a hill in your local park or exploring the jungle that is that untamed bit of your garden? Be as creative as you like to help fuel your child's inner mini-explorer.

FILL YOUR KIT!

There are a million different things you could fill your explorer kit with. Tailor the ideas below to something that you think will really work for your child. Go through the list together and add any other ideas you come up with from around the home. Then fill your case until it's bursting at the seams...

- Magnifying glass
- Binoculars
- String
- Compass
- Tape measure
- Map of your local area
- Camera
- Notepad
- Torch
- Jam jars with vented lids or bug-friendly jars
- Child-friendly scissors
- Candles (that you can pretend are SOS flares)
- Pens and pencils
- Creature-identifying book (for bugs, birds or wildlife)
- Water pistol
- Telescope
- Watch
- Whistle
- Small fishing net
- Trowel or small spade

PLACES TO EXPLORE

There are lots of places you can take your child out to explore — some good places are the garden, a nearby park or forest, or a river or pond close by. Woods and forests are such magical places for children — there are so many unfamiliar sights and sounds and it feels like you're just one wrong footstep from entering a Grimm's fairy tale!

BECOME AN EXPLORER!

There are lots of ways that you and your child can have fun with exploring. Below are just a few suggestions for explorer games.

BUG EXPLORER

Explore any local greenery armed with your magnifying glass and some bug jars! You can try digging for worms or collect some bugs from flowers or under rocks. For older children, bring along a bug-identification book and get them to search out which bugs they've discovered. Once the bugs have been discovered, capture the creepy-crawlies in the bug jars and get your child to draw a sketch in their notebook. Before you go, release the bugs back to their natural environment.

UNDERWATER EXPLORER

Ponds and rivers are filled with interesting wildlife that your child will want to explore. Using the jam jars filled with pond water and a small fishing net, children can investigate any creatures they find, such as tadpoles, bugs, snails, and small fish. Take along a water-creature-identification guide to help educate older children about what they find. Children will need to be accompanied at all times by the water.

ANIMAL TRACKER EXPLORER

Encourage your child to find out about the secret life of animals by exploring their tracks. In your garden, place a folded white sheet in an area where you think animals might visit. Place some food, such as fruit or vegetable peelings, in the middle of the sheet then sprinkle some fresh earth around all the edges of the sheet. Weight the sheet down at the corners with stones. Before nightfall, thoroughly wet the sheet and the earth with a watering can or hose.

DAD TIP

Make sure that your child doesn't damage any of the wildlife during their explorations, to encourage a positive relationship with nature.

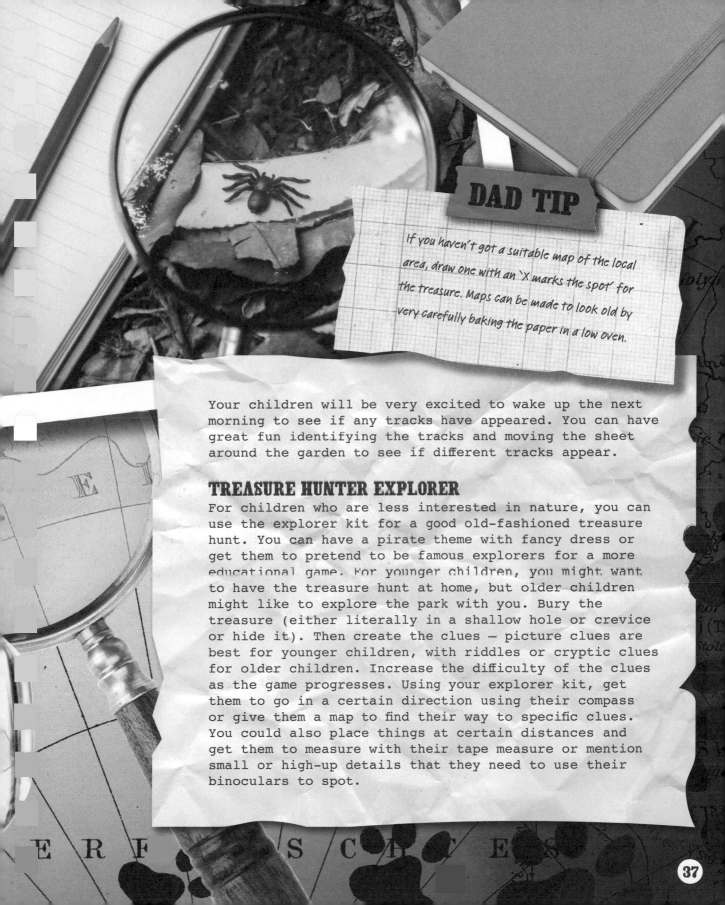

Your children will be very excited to wake up the next morning to see if any tracks have appeared. You can have great fun identifying the tracks and moving the sheet around the garden to see if different tracks appear.

TREASURE HUNTER EXPLORER

For children who are less interested in nature, you can use the explorer kit for a good old-fashioned treasure hunt. You can have a pirate theme with fancy dress or get them to pretend to be famous explorers for a more educational game. For younger children, you might want to have the treasure hunt at home, but older children might like to explore the park with you. Bury the treasure (either literally in a shallow hole or crevice or hide it). Then create the clues — picture clues are best for younger children, with riddles or cryptic clues for older children. Increase the difficulty of the clues as the game progresses. Using your explorer kit, get them to go in a certain direction using their compass or give them a map to find their way to specific clues. You could also place things at certain distances and get them to measure with their tape measure or mention small or high-up details that they need to use their binoculars to spot.

Have A Garden Camp Out

Because you don't need to drive for miles to enjoy a night under the stars.

Going on holiday to an official campsite can be great fun, but your tent doesn't have to sit in a cupboard gathering dust when you're not on holiday. So why not get out that tent and camp out in the garden with your child? It's such a simple way to turn a normal night into an exciting adventure. Your child will love the novelty of sleeping so close yet so far from home and, most importantly of all, it provides a great opportunity to have time away from the distractions of television and computer games indoors. What's more, in your own private garden campsite, there are no boring rules and regulations, no camping charges and hopefully no noisy neighbours...

You will need:
- tent
- bedding
- pyjamas
- torch
- telescope or binoculars (optional)
- some musical instruments
- string
- two tin cans
- screwdriver
- balloons
- football
- apples
- bucket
- garden decorations (optional)

HOW TO MAKE YOUR CAMP OUT EXTRA SPECIAL

PITCHING THE TENT

You could try making the outdoor shelter from page 22 or you could just put up your own tent. Your child will enjoy getting all the tent parts laid out and slotted together, while you hammer in the pegs at the end.

Start your camp-out fun by gathering together all the bedding and nightwear from your house and taking it out to the tent. Get your child to select sleeping positions and set up their bedding for the night ahead.

DECORATE THE GARDEN

You don't have to go crazy, but a few simple decorations could add some atmosphere to your garden. Try putting a few tea lights in jam jars around the garden or put up some simple bunting between trees and bushes.

TRY SOME OUTDOOR GAMES

Before nightfall, play football, charades, catch, tag, apple bobbing or hide and seek. Make sure that everyone has had a really good run around so that the chance of them actually falling asleep is much higher!

HAVE WATER-BOMB FUN

Balloons filled with water can really bring the laughter to a garden campsite, particularly on a really hot summer's evening. And remember, if things get too silly, you can just run away back into the safety of your home to dry off!

TALK ON TIN-CAN TELEPHONES

By connecting two cans to a piece of string, you can make an old-school telephone to talk from one end of the garden to the other. Dad should create a hole in the bottom of each can using a screwdriver, drill or hammer and tie a string between the cans.

STAR GAZE

If you've got a telescope or binoculars bring them, but on a clear night you can really enjoy the stars even with the naked eye. See what constellations you can spot or try to find the

International Space Station. Draw maps of the stars you can see and make up names to remember them by for the next time you adventure in the great outdoors.

GO NOCTURNAL ANIMAL SPOTTING

Try and spot signs of the animals that only come out at night. Listen out for owls, foxes, badgers and more. If you have a pet cat, you'll probably be amazed at how active they are once darkness falls in your garden.

SING SONGS

You might feel silly at first, but once the songs get going you'll have some real fun. And don't just stick to the classic camp-out songs. Who needs 'Kumbaya' or 'Old MacDonald', when the camp can be rocked with a little 'Bohemian Rhapsody' or some One Direction?

TELL STORIES

If your children are young or particularly sensitive, you might want to avoid ghost stories and just do some simple storytelling games. Come up with an opening sentence to a story and then get the child to continue the tale in an imaginative way. Examples could be 'When the aliens invaded earth…' or 'The wizard had just discovered a new special power…'. For older children, have fun with ghost stories. Place a torch under your face and share some scary tales! Obviously don't make them so scary that your children want to run away and hide back in your home. Always try to keep your ghost stories lighthearted so that your children know that they're just a bit of fun and not something to have nightmares over.

MAKE HAND SHADOWS

All you need is a torch and the canvas of your tent. Anybody can do a rabbit, but see if you can shape your hands to make a duck, a rooster, a bear and a butterfly.

DAD TIP

You can create the outdoor shelter that is described on page 22 during the daytime if you want a whole day of outdoor fun.

DAD TIP

If your children are young, bring their teddy bears outside for the camp out; it will make the adventure all the more magic.

We're Going On A Scavenger Hunt

Head outside to search in your garden and beyond...

A scavenger hunt is a great way to let kids safely explore their local environment whilst having some real fun. It couldn't be easier — all you need is to create a list of items to scavenge for and then head outside. People get confused between a treasure hunt and a scavenger hunt but there is a difference. Treasure hunts involve following clues to find hidden treasure, whereas a scavenger hunt involves finding a list of items within a certain time frame.

The trick is to get really hands-on with the nature around you as you hunt and encourage your child to do the same. Touch, sight, smell, sound — get all your child's senses going, as you collect a bounty of pine cones, snail shells, feathers, wild flowers and more.

It doesn't matter whether you live in the countryside or in the heart of a busy town as there's often nature lurking wherever you are. Make the hunt as exciting as it is educational by rummaging around looking for secrets hiding in hedgerows, under rocks and amongst the greenery of your neighbourhood. Just follow these simple steps and get on the scavenger hunt trail!

Remember that if you have more than one child doing the hunt, you will need to make sure they do the activity as a team so you can carefully supervise everyone or take along a few other adults.

You will need:
- pencil
- paper
- wax crayons
- jam jar
- tape measure
- camera phone or camera

CREATE YOUR CHECKLIST

Before you head out, draw a grid on a piece of A4 paper with three horizontal lines (7.5 cm/3 inches apart) and two vertical lines (7.5 cm/3 inches apart). This will give you twelve boxes to fill with the following ideas. Write each one in the space of the box, perhaps drawing a little illustration of each of the highlighted words to help the list really come to life for your little one:

- Collect some **grass** and earth in your jar
- Make a bark rubbing from a **tree** with your crayons
- Find an animal's **footprint** or tracks
- Collect a **feather**
- Hear a **bird** song then try to whistle or sing it
- Smell a wild **flower**
- Find a **snail**'s shell
- Spot a **bird**'s nest in a tree
- Collect a **pine cone**
- Capture a **bug** in your jar
- Count the rings on a **tree stump**
- Find and feel a shiny, smooth **stone**.

For slightly older children, you might want to replace some of the items with the following more challenging suggestions:

- Find a twig shaped like a 'Y'
- Draw something beginning with 'B' that you see
- Take a peek inside an animal's burrow
- Use a tape measure to measure the width of a tree trunk
- Find an item that you can recycle
- Take a photo of your reflection in some water.

DAD TIP

Why not turn the pine cone you collect into a bird feeder when you get home? Simply tie a ribbon to the pine cone, cover it in peanut butter and hang it from a tree. Birds cannot resist!

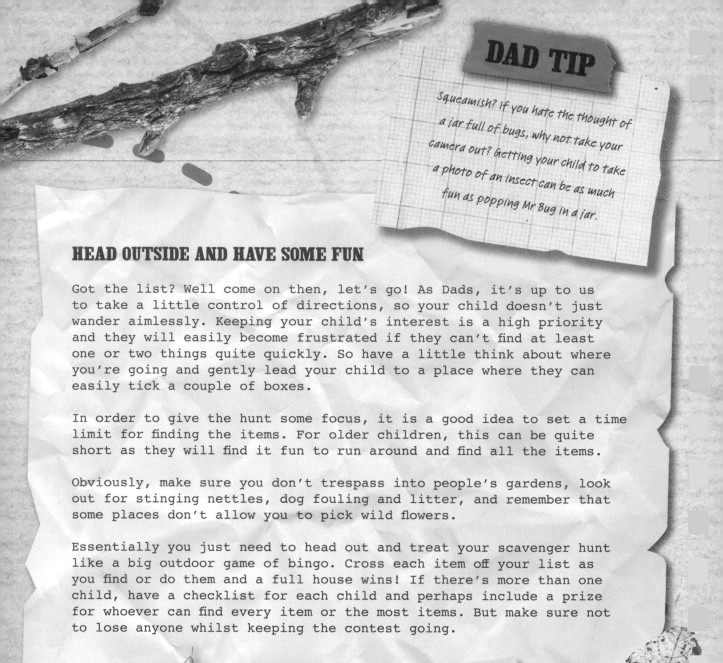

HEAD OUTSIDE AND HAVE SOME FUN

Got the list? Well come on then, let's go! As Dads, it's up to us to take a little control of directions, so your child doesn't just wander aimlessly. Keeping your child's interest is a high priority and they will easily become frustrated if they can't find at least one or two things quite quickly. So have a little think about where you're going and gently lead your child to a place where they can easily tick a couple of boxes.

In order to give the hunt some focus, it is a good idea to set a time limit for finding the items. For older children, this can be quite short as they will find it fun to run around and find all the items.

Obviously, make sure you don't trespass into people's gardens, look out for stinging nettles, dog fouling and litter, and remember that some places don't allow you to pick wild flowers.

Essentially you just need to head out and treat your scavenger hunt like a big outdoor game of bingo. Cross each item off your list as you find or do them and a full house wins! If there's more than one child, have a checklist for each child and perhaps include a prize for whoever can find every item or the most items. But make sure not to lose anyone whilst keeping the contest going.

DAD TIP

A scavenger hunt is a great way to encourage recycling. If you find a lot of litter on your search, use a plastic bag and show your child how people who love nature deal with their waste.

WHY NOT?

Use some of the items from your scavenger hunt in a nature scrapbook (see page 46).

Create A Nature Scrapbook

Scrapbooking is a great way to get your kids into being creative, whilst preserving some memories at the same time.

You will need:

- spiral- or ring-bound scrapbook with thick paper
- nature image printouts
- wax crayons
- glue stick or sticky tape
- felt-tip pens
- colouring pencils
- child-friendly scissors
- old newspapers and magazines
- glitter
- sticky-back plastic
- A4 sheets of paper
- materials collected on walks, such as photos, dried leaves, twigs, feathers, dried flowers, etc.

The first rule of scrapbooking is that there are no rules of scrapbooking. The second rule of scrapbooking is there... are... no... rules of scrapbooking. A scrapbook can be whatever you want it to be — just get involved and fill it with leaves, bark rubbings, photos, anything and everything.

The key is to get a good scrapbook to start off with. You're going to want to really fill this scrapbook with glue, photos, sticky tape and more, so invest in something that at least feels like it isn't going to fall apart at the first sight of a glue stick. It is probably a good idea to get a spiral- or ring-bound scrapbook as this is easiest to lay out flat as you and your child work on the pages.

You can put together your scrapbook however you want, but here are some suggestions for how you could fill the pages.

CREATE A BACKGROUND

To start off your nature scrapbook, you will need to create backgrounds for the pages. You can either get your child to print off a large image that you have found together online — images that make good backdrops include grass, sunsets, the sky. Or you could get your child to draw a background, using crayons to draw images of flowers, grass etc. to cover the page. You can create different backgrounds for each page and you can either do all the backgrounds at once or do them as you create each page.

STICK IN SOME PHOTOS

To add to your nature scrapbook, a good place to start is with a good assortment of photos of things you have seen out on your adventures. Get your child to try their luck at nature photography and see if they can snap any local wildlife in action. To give them a helping hand, take feed to bribe local ducks with or carrots for horses that you know live nearby. Squirrels will sometimes pose for photos if you have a selection of nuts to bribe them with! Once the photos are printed, get your child to cut them out carefully and stick them into the scrapbook. You can either use photo corners or just glue them straight onto the page. Ask your child to annotate each photo with entertaining captions of what the image is, where it was taken and why they like the picture.

MAKE A NATURE COLLAGE

Not all the photos have to be your own. Find some old magazines and newspapers and cut out any pictures you see of wildlife, rivers and plants that your child likes. Get them to paste them into your scrapbook, label each picture and add things like glitter to really bring the pages to life.

When sticking things in, avoid placing glue in the centre as it can warp the surface and create craters on your page.

ADD REAL PLANTS

A great way to preserve and display all the dried leaves, twigs, dried flowers and feathers you have collected on your scavenger hunt (see page 42) is with a collage for your scrapbook. To do this you will need two sheets of sticky-back plastic — you will need to help your child if they find this tricky. Tape the non-sticky side of a sheet to a table, so the sticky side is facing up. Then place all of the nature goodies you want to display onto the sheet. Remove the tape and stick a second sheet on top, sticky side up, then turn it over and press it firmly down into your scrapbook.

ADD A JOURNAL OR POEM

On a separate sheet of paper get your child to write down what they particularly love about a certain aspect of nature. If they can't think of something off the top of their head, help them out and suggest they write about what they would do if they ever saw a grizzly bear in their garden. Cut this out and stick it in.

ADD SKETCHES AND RUBBINGS

Fill your scrapbook with sketches of the insects you catch each night in your bug hotel (see page 18). Make bark rubbings by placing a sheet of paper over the top of a tree bark and rubbing it with a wax crayon.

CREATE THEMED PAGES

A good way to keep your child's interest is to get them to introduce themes to the pages. Some suggestions are: My favourite flowers; My favourite things in the park; My favourite things in the garden; Animals I would like to see in real life; My favourite nature facts.

Encourage your child to be creative — get them to use a variety of colours and textures and to use a mixture of words and images.

DAD TIP

If you have access to a photocopier, it's a great way of keeping your original photos safe from glue!

Let's Go Fly A Kite

This is an incredibly easy kite to make and it can be decorated with your own designs.

You will need:

- 1 x A3 sheet of paper
- ruler
- pencil
- stapler
- hole punch
- 80-cm/32-inch length of thin ribbon
- 60-cm/24-inch length of wide ribbon
- scissors
- ball of thin string
- felt-tip pens, crayons or paints, to decorate as you wish

 Time to make: about 30 minutes

Step 1:

Take an A3 sheet of paper in a colour of your choice and decorate it with felt-tip pens and crayons on both sides. Fold the paper in half widthways, making sure the shortest edges meet at the top.

Step 2:

With the creased edge at the bottom, facing towards you, measure 6.5 cm/2½ inches from the right-hand edge and mark with a pencil. Measure another 6.5 cm/2½ inches from the first pencil mark and mark again with a pencil.

6.5 cm /2½ inch

Step 3:

With the creased edge at the bottom, curl over the top layer of paper so that the top right-hand corner meets the first pencil mark. Hold it in place with your finger.

Step 4:

Pick up the paper, still holding the first corner in place and curl over the other side to meet the same pencil mark.

Pinch together between finger and thumb and staple the two sides together, making sure not to catch your fingers in the stapler.

Step 5:

Use a hole punch to punch a hole at the second pencil mark. Be careful not to punch the hole too close to the edge of the paper.

Step 6:

With a ruler and pencil, take one end of the thin ribbon and make six marks at 10-cm/4-inch intervals along the length of the ribbon. There should still be an unmarked length of 20 cm/ 8 inches at the end.

Step 7:

⚠ Cut the wide ribbon into six shorter lengths, each measuring 10 cm/4 inches. Tie these short ribbons around the thin ribbon in a small knot at each of the marked intervals.

Step 8:

Use the stapler to staple one end of the thin ribbon to the opposite end of the creased fold.

Step 9:

Thread the string through the hole you created with the hole punch. Tie the string in a loose loop (not too tight otherwise the string will cut the paper).

Step 10:

It's time to fly your kite. You'll need a good breeze, but not too windy or your kite might just blow away!

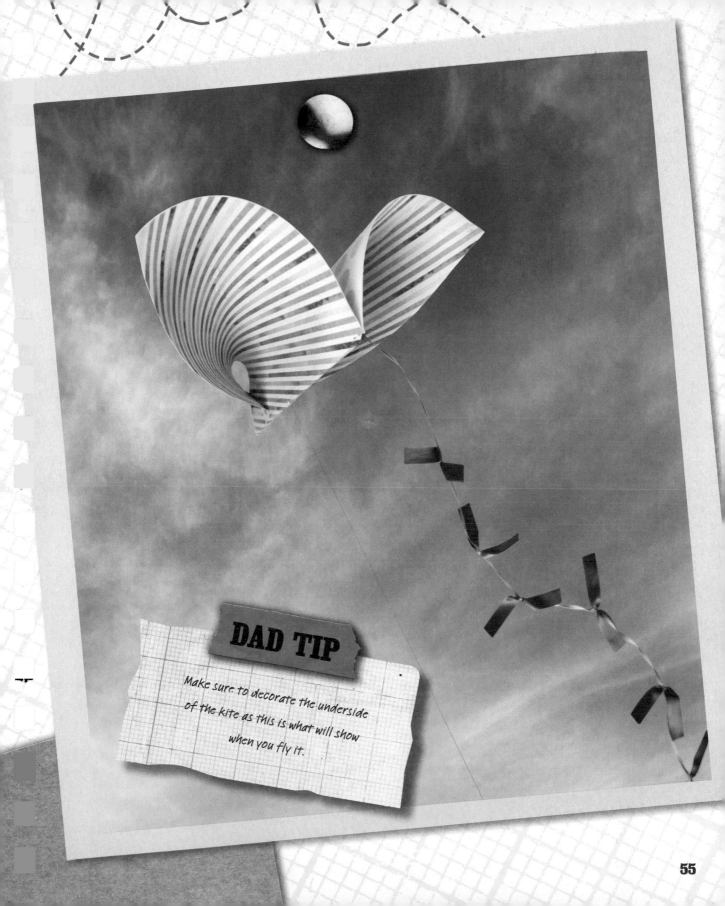

DAD TIP

Make sure to decorate the underside of the kite as this is what will show when you fly it.

A Day At The Beach

Skimming stones and collecting as many shiny seashells as your pockets will hold – the beach is such a very special place for Dad and child.

Close your eyes. Think of a great day out from your own childhood. Chances are you just saw the golden sand of a beach, ice creams melting as fast as you could eat them, and noisy seagulls all playing out to a soundtrack of roaring waves. Yes, the seaside dominates so many of our great childhood memories and the beach really can be such a magical place for children. To make a day out at the coast extra special, it can be a great idea to pack in some really fun activities, such as beachcombing, rock pooling, sand building or fossil hunting. Here are some ideas on how to turn a day beside the seaside with Dad into memories that will last forever.

You will need:
- bucket
- spade
- waterproof non-slip footwear
- plastic containers
- small fishing net
- fossil-identification guide
- empty fizzy drink bottles
- scissors

GO BEACHCOMBING

From coins to shells to lost buckets and spades, there's a whole bounty of hidden treasure buried just underneath the sand. Beachcombing is like the ultimate treasure hunt — so simply start exploring. Dig through the sand, sieve it with your fingers or with a small-holed fishing net and fill a plastic container with what you find. This is best done at the coastline during a low or receding tide or right after a storm, as this is when you find the most treasures. Once you're done, why not take your treasure home? Pebbles, shells, driftwood and feathers all make brilliant things to paint on a rainy day when you wish you were still by the sea.

GO ROCK POOLING

For successful rock pooling, search out rocky areas on sandy or stony seashores that are fairly sheltered. Other sheltered areas, such as underneath piers, can also provide good places for rock pooling. It is best to go at low tide — consult a tide table or guide and head to the area about 30 minutes before low tide so you have plenty of time for collecting. Carefully look under rocks and in pools, using a plastic container filled with seawater to collect any creatures. Make sure you change the water regularly and keep different creatures separate to avoid fighting. Respect the marine life — you should never kill or take a live animal with you. Carefully supervise your child at all times — remember that some creatures have claws and rocks can be slippery so waterproof shoes with good grip are essential.

FOSSIL HUNTING

Beaches are great places for you and your children to find fossils. You can find fossils either along the coastline or among clusters of rocks. Sandy areas, close to where the tide has just gone out, are a good place to start looking. Ammonites (the spiral snail-like shells) are the

DAD TIP

Sturdy, waterproof footwear is essential when climbing on rocks as they can be very slippery and potentially sharp.

most probable find, but do a little online research before you head out to see what fossils might be in your region and where might be the best spot to find them. Depending on where you're looking, you could find the fossils of dinosaur footprints, bones, shark teeth, snails, fish and more. Take along a bucket or plastic container to collect your finds. You could bring a fossil-identification guide with you or research when you get home to discover what sorts of fossils you have found. As with rock pooling, careful supervision and sturdy shoes are essential.

BUILD A SANDMAN

We've all built sandcastles, but why not branch out and build a sandman? A sandman looks like a snowman, but, obviously, is made out of wet sand. Make three balls out of wet sand — a large, medium and small ball. Place the medium ball on top of the larger ball then add the small ball on top. Decorate the sandman, using pebbles for eyes and a mouth, a twig or driftwood for a nose and arms, and seaweed for hair.

MAKE A NATURAL PADDLING POOL

A quick and easy way to have fun on the beach is to dig out a paddling pool in the sand. All you need is a bucket and spade and the energy to dig! Start digging out a small, circular hole, a short distance from the sea. The hole should be wide enough for your child to stand and easily move around in. Place the sand that you dig out around the edge of the circle so that it forms a natural wall around the edge of your pool. Dig down until you hit water and fill the pool slightly with more water from a bucket until you have enough water for your child to paddle in. Don't dig down too deep — your child should only be up to their knees in the hole when they're standing up, so go nearer to the sea if you have to dig deeper before you hit water.

MAKE A SANDCASTLE WATER FOUNTAIN

Help your child to build a sandcastle that becomes a really impressive water fountain!

Step 1:

⚠ Collect a few empty fizzy drinks bottles. Clean them out, remove the labels and screw the lids on. Cut each bottle in half, straight across the middle, using sharp scissors. Both halves are going to act like little 'buckets' to hold the water.

Step 2:

⚠ Using scissors or another sharp implement, make two small holes near the bottom of each bucket — about 5 cm/2 inches up from the bottom and at least 2.5 cm/1 inch apart from each other.

Step 3:

Build a large sandcastle, piled high into the shape of a mountain. Place a bucket at the top of the sandcastle, burying the base securely into the sand but making sure the holes are kept clear. Then place two buckets below the holes of the top bucket, so that the water will cascade out of each hole into the open tops of the two buckets below. Arrange all the other buckets down the sandcastle so that the water flows from one bucket to another, all the way down to the bottom of the sandcastle.

Step 4:

Get your child to collect some seawater and pour the water into the bucket at the top. Watch the water cascade down all the buckets to the bottom. Your child will have lots of fun topping up the fountain with seawater, again and again. And there's no limit to how big and intricate you can make the arrangement of the fountain.

DAD TIP

Sea glass can be taken home to make a great mosaic. It's usually very safe for children as the ocean wears away any sharp edges, but check before giving to your child.

FUN AT HOME

Have fun around the house with these **10** exciting activities!

Drawbridge Castle

This castle, with its own working drawbridge, will be the talk of the town.
Just add a princess or a knight in shining armour to bring it to life.

You will need:

- 1 x large, square, double-thickness, corrugated cardboard box
- glue gun and craft glue
- parcel tape
- craft knife
- scissors
- marker pen
- ruler
- 2 x large crafting lolly sticks
- ball-point pen
- 2 x 1.5-m/4 ft 11-inch lengths of parcel string
- 1 x large 2-cm/¾-inch wooden bead
- 2 x large rectangular, double-thickness, corrugated cardboard boxes
- 2 x large postal tubes
- 1 x about 2-m/6 ft 6-inch length of thick ribbon
- coloured card or paper
- stapler
- paints and paintbrush, to decorate as you wish (optional)

DAD TIP

You can use any size of box for this project, depending on what is available and how big you want the castle to be. Double-thickness cardboard boxes of the type used for storage would be ideal. As an indicator, the boxes for the tall towers need to be as high as just below the chin of the child you are making it for.

Time to make:
1 hour

Step 1:
⚠ Glue the base of the square cardboard box closed with a glue gun. Hold the flaps in place with parcel tape, while the glue sets.

Step 2:
⚠ Turn the box on its side and cut off one flap from the open end with a craft knife or scissors, then cut off the opposite side flap to leave only two flaps opposite each other.

Step 3:
Using a marker pen, draw the shape of a drawbridge on one side of the box that still has a flap attached. Leave a border on both sides of the drawbridge, rather than making it the full width of the box.

⚠ Cut out the shape using a craft knife, but make sure you leave the drawbridge attached along the bottom edge so it's hinged.

Step 4:

Draw three evenly spaced squares with a marker pen and ruler to meet the top edge of one of the flaps, as a guide to cutting out castellations.

⚠ Cut out the squares with a craft knife and repeat on the other flap. Keep the little squares you cut out to use later.

Step 5:

Turn the box over so that the side with the drawbridge is on the floor. Draw an arch on top of the box, making it big enough for your child to crawl through.

⚠ Cut out the arch with a craft knife, removing it completely, as it doesn't need to hinge. Keep the card cut from the arch to use later.

Step 6:

⚠ Glue two large lolly sticks to the top of the drawbridge at a 45-degree angle and half covering the top of the curve. Carefully push a ball-point pen into the box behind the lolly sticks to create two holes that are covered by the ends of the sticks when the drawbridge is closed. Tie one of the lengths of parcel string around one of the crafting lolly sticks. Repeat with the other length of string on the second crafting lolly stick.

Step 7:

Push the ends of the string through the holes to the inside of the box and through the hole in the wooden bead. With the drawbridge completely open, slide the bead down the string until the string is taut. Tie the two loose ends together as close to the bead as you can get and trim the ⚠ excess string with a pair of scissors. Pull the strings to raise the drawbridge, then slide the bead up the string to hold the drawbridge closed.

Step 8:

⚠ To make a tower, glue down the bottom flaps of one of the large, rectangular boxes, holding the flaps in place with parcel tape while the glue sets. Turn the box so the open flaps are at the top. Draw three evenly spaced squares with a marker pen and ruler to meet the top edge of one of the flaps, as a guide to cutting out castellations.

Cut out the squares with a craft knife and repeat on the other flaps. Again, keep the little squares you cut out to use later.

Step 9:

Decide which side will be the back of the tower. Use the piece of arch-shaped card, reserved from step 5, as a template to draw around and cut another arch from the back of this box.

Step 10:

Remove the ends from the postal tubes and mark a line roughly halfway down one of them. Draw two parallel lines, about 5 cm/2 inches apart, down to the end of the tube from this mark.

⚠ Very carefully cut out this section using a craft knife. Be very careful as the tube is quite tough.

Step 11:

⚠ Place the tube over the outside corner of the tower so the cut-out in the tube sits neatly on the edge. Hold and glue in place.

Step 12:

To make the roof for the top of the round tower, cut an arrow shape out of a spare piece of cardboard, making the stem of the arrow the same width as the inside of the tube. Add some craft glue to the sides and slot it into the top of the tube.

Step 13:

Draw a window at the front of the tower. Any shape or size will do, but make sure it's at the right height for your child to see out of.

⚠ Cut it out with a craft knife. Repeat steps 8 to 13 for the other tower, this time gluing the postal tube to the opposite side of the tower.

Step 14:

⚠ Arrange the three boxes so that the central box with the drawbridge is set back a little and glue them together at the sides. Glue the reserved pieces of square card around the windows and drawbridge to create the look of stonework.

Step 15:

⚠ To make the bunting, cut a length of ribbon that is slightly longer than the distance between the tops of the round towers. Cut triangles from coloured card or paper and staple to the top edges to the ribbon. Finally, staple the ends of the bunting to the very tops of the round towers.

Step 16:

Add more round towers, flags and windows and decorate as you like.

Pop-pom Puppy

This pom-pom puppy has adorable droopy ears and a cute collar that can be adapted to any colour ribbon or shape of bead that you wish.

You will need:

- thick black wool (body: approx. 35 g/1¼ oz: head: approx. 25 g/ 1 oz: binding for head and body: 80 cm/32 inches)

- 1 x 12-cm x 7-cm/4½-inch x 2¾-inch piece of cardboard

- sharp scissors

- wool needle

- glue

- templates from page 124

- black felt

- brown felt

- black embroidery thread

- 1 x black plastic nose

- 2 x black plastic eyes

- yellow ribbon

- 1 x red star button

Time to make: about 30 minutes

Step 1:

Wrap the black wool for the body around the cardboard. Wrap it around with consistent and gentle tension, making sure it is not too tight, and wrap it evenly along the length of the cardboard. The wool shouldn't be fatter in the middle. Tuck the last bit of wool into the wool wrap. Gently slide the bundle of wool off the cardboard, making sure you keep hold so it doesn't unravel. Using a piece of wool, 30 cm/12 inches long, wrap the wool around the bundle horizontally, making sure it is tight. It will squeeze the wrapped wool together in the middle.

⚠ Slide the blade of your scissors into the loops of the bundle and gradually work your way around, until you have a rough pom-pom.

Step 2:

⚠ Repeat Step 1 for the puppy's head, using less wool to create a slightly smaller pom-pom. Trim the smaller pom-pom to form a neat round shape for the puppy's head. Trim the larger pom-pom to create the puppy's body so that it has a flat top and body and straighter sides.

Step 3:

⚠ Using a large needle threaded with wool, 20 cm/8 inches long, thread the needle through the bottom of the body and up through the head. Loop the wool back through the top of the head and through the body, then tie in a knot at the bottom to hold them together. You can also dab glue between the head and the body to make it extra secure before sewing.

Photocopy or trace the templates on page 124. Using the template as a guide, cut out the puppy's ears from the black felt. Pinch the flat edge of the ears to form a pleat and, using a needle and black thread, sew in place.

Step 4:

Add glue to the pinched edge of the ears and wedge the ears into the side of the pom-pom head so that they droop downwards.

Step 5:

Using the templates on page 124, cut out the puppy's nose from brown felt. Cut a little hole in the nose and insert the black bead nose. Add a black vertical stitch to the felt underneath the nose. Glue the black beads for the eyes and the nose to the puppy's head. Leave to dry.

Step 6:

Using the template on page 124 as a guide, cut out the puppy's feet from the black felt. Wedge the paws near the base of the body pom-pom so that they droop down a little, rather than stick them to the bottom of the pom-pom. Finally, glue the red star button in place on the ribbon, wrap it around the puppy's neck and glue at the back.

DAD TIP

This cute pom-pom puppy is not suitable for children under 3 years of age, so only give this to older children.

Or you could...

Make the puppy's body from two different shades of wool.
Draw a line halfway down the cardboard to act as a guide.
Wrap half the cardboard with white wool and the other half
with black wool. Trim the pom-pom so the white part is
smaller than the black, to give him a white tummy.

Catapult Game

Become a pro at aiming with a catapult and target made from recycled materials.

 Time to make:
1 hour

You will need:

- 2 x about 30-cm/12-inch long cardboard tubes (from inside kitchen foil or clingfilm)
- ruler
- felt-tip pen
- chopping board
- ball-point pen
- parcel tape
- small plastic dessert pot
- 2 x paper cups
- 1 x 8-mm/½-inch diameter, 20-cm/8-inch long wooden dowel (or similar, such as a chopstick)

- PVA glue or glue gun or double-sided sticky tape
- cereal box
- craft knife
- scissors
- 1 x toilet roll tube, cut in half to make two small tubes
- 2 x 15-cm/6-inch long, large crafting lolly sticks
- paint, pens, paintbrushes, to decorate as you wish
- newspaper or magazine
- small plastic milk carton (optional)

Step 1:

Using a ruler, measure 10 cm/4 inches in from the left end of one of the cardboard tubes and make a mark with the felt-tip pen. Make a further four marks at 2-cm/¾-inch intervals. ⚠ Place the cardboard tube on a hard flat surface, such as a chopping board, and hold securely with one hand. Using the ball-point pen, carefully push and twist the pen nib into the first 10-cm/4-inch pen mark until you break through the tube. Rotate the pen so it makes a nice round hole. Repeat this on the remaining four pen marks.

Step 2:

⚠ Hold the end of the tube, making sure the holes are nowhere near your hand. Push the ball-point pen into the first hole and gently twist and push so you start to make a hole in the opposite side of the tube. Push the pen right through the tube and rotate to make a nice hole. Repeat this on the remaining holes, making sure your hand stays clear of the potential exit holes.

Step 3:

Tape the dessert pot to the other end of the cardboard tube with parcel tape. Make sure the holes on the tube line up horizontally with the side of the pot. Stick two pieces of tape either side of the pot, then wrap a longer length of tape around the end of the tube. Add one more short piece to tape the bottom of the pot to the tube, finally wrapping one more long piece around the ends of the tape on the tube. Make sure the tape is securely stuck down. Put to one side.

Step 4:

⚠ Take one of the paper cups and hold it upside-down. Use the ball-point pen to make a hole in the side about 1 cm/½ inch away from the bottom of the cup. Mind your hands. Continue to push the pen through the cup and out the opposite side. Twist the pen to make the hole round. Repeat on the other paper cup.

Step 5:

Push the dowel through one set of holes in the cardboard tube so that it sits with equal amounts protruding on either side. Now push the paper cups onto the ends of the dowel. The catapult is ready.

Step 6:

Either glue or use double-sided tape to seal the ends of the cereal box closed. Place it flat on a table so the back of the box is face down. Draw a line with a felt-tip pen and a ruler that is 3 cm/1¼ inches in from the left short edge, right short edge and top long edge and a line 5 cm/2 inches up from the bottom long edge.

⚠ Use a craft knife to cut out the panel from the centre of the box. Be very careful when you do this, the box could collapse so press gently. Keep the card you cut out.

Step 7:

Turn the box over. Draw a line with a felt-tip pen and ruler 3 cm/1¼ inches in from the left short edge and right short edge and a line 5 cm/2 inches up from the bottom long edge. This time you don't need a line across the top.

⚠ Use a craft knife to cut out the panel from the centre of the box, cutting along the top crease line of the box so that there isn't a border across the top. You may find it easier to cut the top edge with a pair of scissors.

Step 8:

Place the box on one of its shorter ends, the larger border closest to you and the larger frame area to your right. On the top of the box, draw a line 2 cm/¾ inch in from the left long edge and a line 1 cm/½ inch up from the bottom short edge with a felt-tip pen and ruler. Place one end of the remaining cardboard tube in the middle of the two lines. Draw around the tube with a felt-tip pen to make a circle the size of the tube.

Step 9:

⚠ Using the craft knife, very carefully cut the hole out. The box is quite unstable at the ends, so don't press too heavily and keep your fingers clear at all times. Reseal the edges with double-sided tape or glue, if necessary. Repeat the previous step on the opposite end of the box to create two holes that line up directly opposite each other.

Step 10:

Start to feed the cardboard tube into one end of the box through the hole you just made. As you do so, feed the two halves of the toilet roll onto it before pushing the cardboard tube through the opposite side of the box. You should have equal amounts of tube protruding either side of the box.

Step 11:

⚠️ Lay the box flat on the table with the side that has the frame on all four sides facing down. Take a lolly stick and glue it to one toilet roll half on the side nearer to the frame at the bottom, making sure the top of the stick is covering the top frame. This is a bit fiddly, so take your time and check you have set it up correctly before applying the glue. Repeat for the other lolly stick and toilet roll half.

Step 12:

When the box is upright, the lolly sticks should rest against the frame on the inside front of the box, as shown in the image.

Step 13:

Place one of the pieces of reserved card, cut from the box earlier, plain side up on a table. Using a roll of parcel tape as a guide, draw two circles on the card with a felt-tip pen.

⚠️ Cut out the circle using either scissors or the craft knife. If you are using a craft knife, make sure to protect the table top with a chopping board or spare piece of card.

Step 14:

Glue the discs to the front of the lolly sticks so they sit centrally in the box window.

Now, it's time to decorate your catapult and target box with paint, pens or whatever you choose.

Step 15:

To make the projectiles, scrunch up a sheet of newspaper as tightly as you can. Try not to make the ball any bigger than the size of a golf ball.

DAD TIP

How to play:

Position your target box on the floor, a couple of metres away from you with the targets upright. Next, place your newspaper ball projectile into the plastic cup on the catapult. With one hand, hold one of the stands firmly. Take aim at the target and smack down on the end of the cardboard tube. Don't hit too hard or you'll squash the tube. Try to knock down the targets. Try adjusting the catapult to see how far your projectile will go. Just move the wooden dowel to a different hole position and try again. And remember, aim at a target and not a person.

Variation:

As an alternative to the target, you can make
a 'catcher' out of a plastic milk carton.
⚠ Cut a cube shape from the bottom of the milk
carton leaving the handle and the bottom of
the carton to look like a scoop. Just draw the
cut lines with a permanent marker and then
carefully cut the milk carton with a pair of
scissors. One person catapults while the other
person tries to catch the newspaper balls.

Crusher-bot Puppet

Wreak havoc on the neighbourhood with a Crusher-bot puppet.
You can make his jaws open and close and wiggle his arms.

Time to make:
about 40 minutes

You will need:

- small corrugated cardboard box, about **23 cm/9 inches** wide x **16 cm/6¼ inches** high x **10 cm/4 inches** deep
- ruler
- pencil
- sharp scissors or craft knife
- glue gun or double-sided sticky tape
- ball-point pen
- ball of string
- **6 x table-tennis balls**
- piece of thick corrugated card or small chopping board
- **3 x toilet roll tubes, 4 cm/1½ inches** in diameter
- template from page **126**
- piece of thick corrugated card, about **20 cm/8 inches** square
- **4 x 2-cm/¾-inch** wooden beads
- **1 x tennis ball**
- **1 x large round coin**
- **4 x large crafting lolly sticks**
- **4 x 2-cm/¾-inch** buttons
- **4 x 70-cm/28-inch** lengths of button thread
- paints and paintbrushes, stickers or tissue paper, to decorate as you wish

Step 1:

Remove any tape, along with any stickers or labels, from the top and the bottom of the box. Open up the box, measure and mark with a pencil half the width on the short side of the box and draw a line from the top to the bottom of the box on both sides. Cut along the line with a pair of scissors and repeat on the other side, so the box is in two halves.

Step 2:

⚠ Take one of the box halves and glue the flaps together with either a glue gun or double-sided sticky tape to create an open top box. Repeat with the other box half.

Step 3:

On the front of each box, measure 2 cm/ ¾ inch down from the top open edge and draw a horizontal line with a pencil. Draw an even number of vertical lines, evenly spaced above the line, for the teeth. Mark out the squares you are going to cut out with a diagonal line. ⚠ Using the scissors or craft knife, carefully cut out the alternate squares to look like teeth. Don't worry if they are uneven. Repeat on the other box.

Step 4:

Turn the boxes around so the teeth are facing away from you. Measure 1.5 cm/½ inch down from the top open edge and draw a line across the box width with a pencil. Measure 3 cm/1¼ inches in from both sides and make a mark. Use the ball-point pen to make two small holes through the box. Repeat on the other box.

Step 5:

Place the two boxes on a table, back to back so the holes line up. Cut two pieces of string, about 20 cm/8 inches long. Feed one end of the string through the holes and tie the boxes together with a knot. Repeat with the other piece of string and then trim the excess with scissors. Make sure the loops of string are quite loose so that the jaw opens and closes easily.

Step 6:

Decide which of the two boxes will be the lower jaw and write 'LJ' in small letters on it. Using the ruler and pencil, draw a diagonal line on one of the shortest sides from one corner to the other of the lower jaw. Then draw a diagonal line from the opposite corners — where the lines cross will mark the centre. Using a ball-point pen, make a small hole where the lines cross. Do the same on the other short side of the lower jaw. This is where you will attach the arms. Put to one side.

Step 7:

Place one of the table-tennis balls on a scrap piece of thick card or a chopping board. With either the sharp point of a pair of scissors or a craft knife, make a small hole in the centre that's big enough to thread string through. Be very careful while doing this, making sure to press very gently on the ball as it is very thin. Make a hole on the opposite side of the ball to the first hole.

Step 8:

Cut a 30-cm/12-inch length of string and tie five or six knots at one end to make one large knot. Thread the other end of the string through the two holes in the table-tennis ball.

Glue the table-tennis ball to one end of a toilet roll tube, using the glue gun and making sure the knotted end of the string is inside the toilet roll. Use the glue gun to stick another table-tennis ball to the other end of the toilet roll. Repeat steps 7 and 8 for the other arm.

Step 9:

Photocopy or trace the template on page 126 and using this as a guide, draw two shapes onto a piece of thick corrugated card. Make sure the semi-circle is the same size as the table-tennis balls and that one is a mirror image of the other.

⚠ Use the craft knife and a ruler to carefully cut out the grabbers. Use a glue gun to stick one of the grabbers to the end of one of the table-tennis balls without the string. Glue it at a slight angle rather than straight. Repeat for the opposite arm.

Step 10:

Thread the string from one of the arms through the hole at the side of the lower jaw you made earlier. Thread one of the wooden beads onto the string and tie a knot to hold it in place. Make sure there is enough slack in the string so that the arm dangles down and there is plenty of movement. Repeat on the opposite side.

Step 11:

⚠ Draw a line around the centre of the tennis ball. Put the tennis ball onto a piece of thick corrugated card or chopping board and use a craft knife to very carefully cut it half, using the line as a guide. Take your time over this as tennis balls are quite tough. Cut the remaining toilet roll tube in half using either the scissors or craft knife to create two equal-length tubes. Use the glue gun to stick one of the tubes to the top of half a tennis ball. Repeat for the other half of the tube and ball.

Step 12:

Turn the Crusher-bot head upside-down so the lower jaw is uppermost.

⚠ Glue the two feet onto the bottom of the jaw with the glue gun, making sure they are in the middle and spaced evenly. Once the glue has set, turn the Crusher-bot the right way up. He should stand quite happily on his own two feet.

Step 13:

Measure the width of the head along the top front edge and make a pencil mark at the halfway point. Use a ball-point pen to make a small hole where the pencil mark is at the top front edge.

Step 14:

Draw a diagonal line from one corner to the opposite corner of the top of the head and then draw another diagonal line between the other two corners to find the centre. Place a large coin in the centre of the top of the head.

⚠ Draw around the coin and then use a craft knife to cut out a hole.

Step 15:

Turn Crusher-bot upside-down. Use a ruler to find the centre and use a ball-point pen to make a small hole in the centre point. Turn Crusher-bot the right way up.

Step 16:

Take the last two table-tennis balls and use the glue gun to stick them to the top front edge of Crusher-bot, making sure they are about 1 cm/½ inch apart. Don't use too much glue otherwise it will drip down the front of the head. Decorate and paint your Crusher-bot however you wish and leave to one side to dry.

Step 17:

⚠ Using the glue gun, add a line of glue along only half of the length of one of the craft lolly sticks. Place another lolly stick on top and press firmly together. Allow the glue to dry completely.

Step 18:

⚠ Gently pull apart the unglued ends of the lolly sticks. Carefully push a wooden bead into the open end, making sure the hole is visible between the sticks, and then use the glue gun to glue it in place. Hold the bead while the glue sets, making sure you don't get any on your fingers. Add a bit more glue to make sure the bead is stuck well in place. Set aside to dry completely.

Step 19:

⚠ Glue the ends of the other two lolly sticks together, overlapping by about 4 cm/1¾ inches. Allow the glue to set before proceeding. Then cut a small 'V' shape about 1 cm/½ inch from the ends of the lolly sticks using a really sharp pair of pointed scissors. Put the sticks to one side.

Step 20:

⚠ Glue the two lolly stick parts together to form a cross, as shown in the diagram. Make sure the two halves are glued really well together. The hole in the bead should be facing upwards.

Step 21:

⚠ Cut four 70-cm/28-inch lengths of button thread. Securely tie a button at the end of each one. Trim any excess thread from the ends.

Step 22:

Open up the head of Crusher-bot. Feed one length of thread and button up through the hole in the middle of the lower jaw, so the button is on the outside. Then continue to feed the string through the large hole in the top of the head. Close the head and pull the string until it stops. Tie the string you've just pulled up through the head, to the centre of the lolly stick cross. Tie it tightly, ⚠ making sure you have only a small amount of excess thread, before trimming it with scissors.

Step 23:

Open up the head again and push a second thread through the small hole between Crusher-bot's eyes. Pull it through until it's stopped by the button. Feed it through the bead on the end of the lolly-stick cross. Tie the last wooden bead to the thread, making sure that when you hold the lolly-stick cross directly above Crusher-bot's head, the bead is hovering about 1 cm/½ inch above the bead that is glued to the cross.

Step 24:

Using the ball-point pen, make a small hole in the outer claw of each grabber. Feed one of the lengths of thread and button through the hole you just made and then tie the other end to the end of the arm of the lolly-stick cross, where you cut the 'V' shape earlier. Repeat on the other arm. When you hold the lolly-stick cross above his head, the arms should hang outstretched. If they are a bit low, just wind the thread around the lolly stick a couple of times and you're done. You can open his jaw by pulling the bead.

Imaginative Questions

Create some interesting questions that you can put in a jar to spark up new conversations with your child.

You will need:
- paper
- scissors
- pencil or knitting needle
- clean jar

When you need five minutes' peace, chances are that your child will be as noisy as a tornado. However, when you do want a conversation and to find out more about their day, for example on their return from school or a sleepover, more often than not they go mute. Questions such as 'What did you do today?' are always met with 'Dunno. I can't remember.'

There is however a great game you can play to spark up new, fun conversations with your child. This involves creating some interesting questions that you put in a jar and pick out at random. We've listed some suggestions here to get you on your way, but you really can put anything in that jar. You can be quite surreal and amusing or choose questions that will get an honest and emotional response.

DAD TIP

To keep interest up, you could put a couple of prize slips in the jar. Instead of a question, notes could say 'YOU WIN...'.

GETTING STARTED

Firstly, get all your questions down on paper. Either handwrite them or type them up and print them off. Once you've done that, cut your questions into little slips. Wrap the slips around a pencil or knitting needle to create a swirl that can be uncurled when you pull the questions out. Put your springy swirls into the jam jar and it's that easy.

WARNING: You may never be able to shut your child up again!

QUESTION IDEAS:

- If you could have a pet alligator, where would you keep him?

- What was the best dream you have ever had?

- If you could be any type of ice cream, what would you be?

- What is the last thing that made you smile?

- How would you describe yourself to someone who hasn't met you?

- What's the biggest dog you've ever seen?

- If you could have a power like a superhero, what power would you like?

- What is the yuckiest thing you've ever eaten?

- What is your greatest dance move?

- If you were a dinosaur, what would you smell like?
- When was the last time you were really muddy?
- If you could re-name yourself, what would you like to be called?
- What is the first thing you can ever remember?
- What is the biggest surprise you've ever had?
- If you were a witch, who would you turn into a toad?
- Where is your favourite place in the world?
- When was the last time you got really silly?
- What is your favourite thing that Mum does with you?
- If you could drive a car, where would you drive to?
- What colour is the happiest colour?
- If you could be any flavour of crisps, what would you be?
- Would you rather travel back in time or through space?
- What's the funniest face you can pull?
- What is your favourite film?
- If you were invisible for a day, what would you do?
- What sound annoys you the most?
- If you could go to the moon, what is the first thing you would do there?
- Would you rather be too hot or too cold?
- Why don't monkeys live in houses?
- Who is the funniest person you know?
- If you were the richest person in the world, what would you do with all your money?
- What's the yuckiest smell you've ever smelt?
- Would you rather be able to fly or be invisible?

- If you could make three wishes, what would they be?
- What is the coolest thing you have ever seen?
- How many hugs do you need every day?
- If you were to put any question in this jar, what would you go for?
- What is your favourite day in the week?
- If you could be any animal, which one would you be?
- What do you want to be when you grow up?
- If you could only keep one toy, which one would you keep?

DAD TIP

You could include some challenges or dares in the jar as well. So, you could write on the slip 'Now, do a star jump!' or 'Name five things beginning with D'.

Get Creative In The Kitchen

Children love to have fun and create in the kitchen — especially if they get to taste the results afterwards! Although half of the effort can involve stopping your child from eating all of the ingredients before they're baked, cooking with your child is a rewarding and entertaining experience. It can also be quite creative if there is decoration involved — your child will love adding edible sparkles and icings to baked cookies and cakes and you can encourage them to choose their favourite colours and shapes to decorate with. Safety is important in the kitchen as well, so make sure your child is kept well away from the oven when it is hot and supervise them closely at all times. Your child will develop an understanding of how food is produced, as well as getting a great treat after all the hard work is done. Get baking!

FIZZY PINK CUPCAKES

You will need:

Makes: 10

- 115 g/4 oz self-raising flour, sifted
- ¼ tsp baking powder
- 115 g/4 oz unsalted butter, cut into small pieces, softened
- 115 g/4 oz caster sugar
- 2 large eggs, lightly beaten
- pink, white and red sprinkles, to decorate
- 10 pink drinking straws, cut to 8 cm/3½ inches long, to serve

Butter icing
- 115 g/4 oz unsalted butter, softened
- 225 g/8 oz icing sugar
- 1 tbsp lemon juice
- pink food colouring

- 10-hole bun tin
- 10 paper cases
- sieve
- large bowl
- electric hand-held mixer
- dessertspoon
- oven gloves
- wire rack
- medium bowl
- palette knife
- plate

Step 1:
⚠ Preheat the oven to 180°C/350°F/Gas Mark 4. Line a bun tin with 10 paper cases. Put the flour and baking powder into a large bowl. Add the butter, caster sugar and eggs and whisk using an electric hand-held mixer until the mixture is pale and fluffy.

Step 2:
⚠ Using a dessertspoon, spoon the mixture into the paper cases. Bake for 15–20 minutes, until risen and golden. Remove from the oven and leave the cupcakes to cool a little. Transfer to a wire rack.

Step 3:
⚠ For the butter icing, beat together the butter, icing sugar and lemon juice in a medium bowl with an electric hand-held mixer. Stir in a little pink food colouring to give a pale pink colour.

Step 4:
Thickly swirl the icing over the tops of the cupcakes using a palette knife. Put the sprinkles on a plate, hold onto the paper cases and roll the cupcake edges in the sprinkles. Push a straw into the top of the cupcakes to decorate.

LAVA VOLCANO CAKES

Makes: 12

You will need:

- 100 g/3½ oz butter, softened, plus extra for greasing
- 100 g/3½ oz caster sugar
- 100 g/3½ oz soft light brown sugar
- 1 large egg
- 1 tsp vanilla extract
- 150 g/5½ oz plain flour
- 25 g/1 oz cocoa powder
- ½ tsp baking powder

Chocolate sauce

- 200 ml/7 fl oz double cream
- 2 tbsp milk
- 100 g/3½ oz plain chocolate, chopped

To serve

- 1 x 600 ml/1 pint tub vanilla ice cream
- gold and silver star sprinkles
- 12 mini candles

- 12-hole muffin tin
- large bowl
- electric hand-held mixer
- sieve
- wooden spoon
- teaspoon
- oven gloves
- palette knife
- wire rack
- small saucepan

Step 1:

Preheat the oven to 180°C/350°F/Gas Mark 4. Grease a 12-hole muffin tin. Place the butter, sugars, egg and vanilla in a large bowl and use an electric hand-held mixer to beat together until the mixture is light and fluffy. Sift over the flour, cocoa and baking powders and stir with a wooden spoon to make a soft dough.

Step 2:

Use a wet teaspoon to divide the mixture into 12 portions and place into the muffin tin holes. Press the mixture up the sides of each of the muffin tin holes — it should look quite rough around the edges.

Step 3:

Bake in the preheated oven for 15–18 minutes or until the cakes are just firm at the edges. Leave to cool in the tin for 5 minutes. Carefully run a palette knife around the edge of each cake to loosen it from the tin. Transfer to a wire rack to cool completely.

Step 4:

To make the 'lava' chocolate sauce, heat the cream and milk together in a small saucepan until almost boiling. Remove from the heat, add the chocolate and stir until a smooth sauce forms. Set aside but keep warm.

Step 5:

To serve, place a warm cake 'volcano' on a plate, top with a scoop of vanilla ice cream and make a 'lava flow' with the chocolate sauce. Sprinkle with gold and silver star sprinkles. Finally, place a candle in the centre of each cake and light carefully. Bring to the table with the candle lit for best effect!

95

DAD TIP

Sparklers or fountain candles would also look great. Choose ones that are especially designed for cakes and keep children at a distance.

SWEETHEART COOKIES

Makes: 32

You will need:
- 200 g/7 oz unsalted butter, softened
- 150 g/5½ oz caster sugar
- 1 large egg
- 2 tsp vanilla extract
- 400 g/14 oz plain flour

Royal icing
- 450 g/1 lb icing sugar
- 15 g/½ oz egg white powder
- 6 tbsp cold water
- 4 food colouring gels, such as bright red, pink, blue and mauve

- 2 large bowls
- electric hand-held mixer
- wooden spoon
- sieve
- clingfilm
- baking paper
- 3 baking sheets
- rolling pin
- selection of heart-shaped cutters
- palette knife
- oven gloves
- wire rack
- 5 small bowls
- cocktail sticks
- piping bag and No. 3 or 4 nozzle
- 4 squeezy icing bottles

Step 1:

⚠ Put the butter and sugar into a large bowl and mix well with an electric hand-held mixer. Beat in the egg and vanilla extract with a wooden spoon. Sift in the flour and mix everything together to make a rough dough. Gather the dough into a ball with your hands, wrap it in clingfilm and chill in the refrigerator for at least 10 minutes.

Step 2:

⚠ Line three baking sheets with baking paper. Unwrap the dough and place between two sheets of baking paper. Roll out to an even thickness of 5 mm/¼ inch, turning the dough occasionally. Press out different-sized cookies using the heart cutters, gathering up the trimmings and re-rolling the dough as necessary.

Step 3:

⚠ Using a palette knife, transfer the cookies onto the lined baking sheets. Chill in the refrigerator for 10 minutes — this will help to prevent them spreading during baking. Meanwhile, preheat the oven to 180°C/350°F/Gas Mark 4.

Step 4:

⚠ Bake for 15—18 minutes in the preheated oven until just turning golden at the edges. Cool on the baking sheets for a few minutes before transferring to a wire rack to cool completely. Lower the oven temperature to 120—140°C/250—275°F/Gas Mark 1/2 —1 to be ready for Step 8.

Step 5:

⚠ To make the royal icing, sift the icing sugar into a large bowl and add the egg white powder and water. Stir with a wooden spoon until thickening and the icing sugar has dissolved. Now use an electric hand-held mixer to beat the icing for 3—4 minutes until it is thick, like toothpaste.

Step 6:

Divide the icing in two and place in two small bowls. Colour one half red by gradually adding food colouring gel with the tip of a cocktail stick and kneading to an even colour, and leave the other white. Spoon a third of the red icing into a piping bag fitted with a No. 3 or 4 plain nozzle. Carefully pipe a red icing border around the edge of each cookie and leave to set for 10 minutes.

Step 7:

To make the 'flood' icing, add water to the white and red icings, a drop at a time and beating between additions, until the icing is the consistency of thick Greek yogurt. Divide the white icing into three and colour each third a different colour. Spoon the icings into squeezy icing bottles fitted with plain nozzles.

Step 8:

⚠ Working on a few cookies at a time, direct the icings inside the piped borders. Then pipe a few spots or lines in the other icing colours and use a cocktail stick to feather the contrasting icing. Gently tap the cookies to make any air bubbles rise to the surface and pop these with a cocktail stick. Repeat with the rest of the cookies and icings. Return the cookies to the low oven and dry out for about 40 minutes or until the icing is set.

DINOSAUR SKELETON COOKIES

You will need:

- 200 g/7 oz unsalted butter, softened
- 150 g/5 oz soft light brown sugar
- 1 large egg
- 2 tbsp black treacle
- 400 g/14 oz plain flour
- ½ tsp ground ginger
- ½ tsp ground cinnamon

Royal icing

- 150 g/5½ oz icing sugar
- 2 tsp egg white powder
- 2 tbsp cold water

- baking paper
- 2 baking sheets
- large bowl
- electric hand-held mixer
- sieve
- wooden spoon
- clingfilm
- rolling pin
- assorted dinosaur cutters
- palette knife
- oven gloves
- wire rack
- medium bowl
- piping bag and No. 2 or 3 nozzle

Step 1:

⚠ Line two baking sheets with baking paper. In a large bowl, cream the butter and sugar with an electric hand-held mixer until just coming together. Add the egg and treacle and briefly whisk together. Sift in the flour, ground ginger and ground cinnamon, and mix with a wooden spoon to make a rough dough. Gather it into a ball with your hands, wrap in clingfilm and chill in the refrigerator for at least 10 minutes.

Step 2:

⚠ Roll out the dough between two large sheets of baking paper to an even thickness of 5 mm/¼ inch, turning the dough occasionally. Press out 28 dinosaur shapes using the cutters, re-rolling the dough as necessary. Using a palette knife, transfer the cookies to the lined baking sheets, leaving a little space between each. Chill in the refrigerator for 10 minutes. Meanwhile, preheat the oven to 180°C/350°F/Gas Mark 4.

Step 3:

⚠ Bake for 15–18 minutes until just turning golden at the edges. Cool on the baking sheets for a few minutes before transferring to a wire rack to cool completely. Reduce the oven temperature to 120–140°C/250–275°F/Gas Mark ½–1 to be ready for Step 5.

DAD TIP

To pipe the skeleton shapes, start with the main bones on each dinosaur, then add the smaller bones for extra detail.

Step 4:

⚠ To make the royal icing, sift the icing sugar and egg white powder into a medium bowl, add the water then use a wooden spoon to gently stir the mixture until all the powder has dissolved. Now use an electric hand-held mixer to beat the mixture for 3–4 minutes until the icing is thick, like toothpaste. Spoon the icing into a piping bag fitted with a No. 2 or 3 piping nozzle and pipe skeleton shapes onto the cookies.

Step 5:

⚠ Place the cookies on baking sheets and dry out in the low oven for about 40 minutes or until nice and hard. Remove from the oven and leave to cool for a few minutes before transferring to a wire rack to cool completely.

Shadow Puppet Theatre

Create your own little characters and put on a show
with this really easy-to-make puppet theatre.

You will need:

- 3 x similar-sized cereal boxes
- double-sided sticky tape
- ruler
- pen or pencil
- craft knife or scissors
- A3 sheet of tracing paper or
  baking paper
- template on page 127
- crafting lolly sticks
- torch or table lamp
- paints, paintbrushes and pens,
  to decorate as you wish

Time to make:
about 30 minutes

Step 1:

Seal up the open end of one of the cereal boxes using double-sided sticky tape. Lay the box flat and draw lines 2 cm/¾ inch in from each edge of the top face of the box with a ruler and pen or pencil. ⚠ Carefully cut out the rectangle using a craft knife or scissors.

Step 2:

Turn the box over and draw lines 2 cm/¾ inch in from one of the long sides and two of the short sides. ⚠ Cut along the lines you've just drawn down to the bottom edge of the box and cut along the bottom edge.

Step 3:

Stick 2-cm/¾-inch lengths of double-sided sticky tape on the four corners of the side of the box with the borders on all four sides. Carefully lay a sheet of tracing paper as flat as possible on top of the box and rub the corners to stick the paper to the tape, making sure the paper doesn't buckle or crease.

Step 4:
⚠️ Trim the sides of the paper to the size of the box.

Step 5:
Open up the second cereal box and lay it out flat on a table with the printed side facing down. Place your theatre box onto the card and draw around the outside with either a pen or pencil. Remove the theatre box and place to one side.

Step 6:
Draw the outline of a theatre front that is bigger than the rectangle you've just drawn. The curtains on the sides should slightly overlap the border of the theatre box.
⚠️ Cut out the theatre front using scissors.

Step 7:

Place the theatre box on a table with the tracing paper facing down and put double-sided sticky tape down the borders of the short sides. Leave the top edge without any sticky tape.

Step 8:

Carefully place the theatre front on top of the box and the sticky tape, keeping it central and lining up the bottom of the theatre front with the bottom of the theatre box.

Step 9:

Open the last cereal box out flat. Measure the height and width of the theatre box. Add 4 cm/1½ inches to the height, take away 4 cm/1½ inches from the width and draw out a rectangular shape with those dimensions onto the flat box. For example, if the theatre box is 20 cm/8 inches high x 30 cm/12 inches wide, draw a rectangle 24 cm/9½ inches high x 26 cm/10½ inches wide. Cut the rectangle out and slide it into the slot between the theatre box and front.

Step 10:

Photocopy or trace the puppet templates on page 127, or draw your own puppet shapes if you prefer, on a spare piece of card. Cut out the puppets with scissors and attach them at the back with double-sided sticky tape to crafting lolly sticks. Decorate the front of the theatre however you wish.

Step 11:

Place your theatre on the edge of a table, in front of a table lamp or torch set up to shine a light behind the theatre. Hold up your puppets behind the tracing paper to cast a shadow and create a shadow puppet show.

DAD TIP

For more ideas on how to be creative with your shadow puppet theatre, see pages 14–15.

Monster Truck

You can't beat a car that you can wear! This mini Monster Truck is made to measure with ribbons that slip over the shoulders.

You will need:

- glue gun
- large, rectangular, corrugated cardboard box
- ruler
- pencil
- craft knife
- ball-point pen
- scissors
- medium, rectangular, corrugated cardboard box
- template for the windscreen on page 125
- large cereal box, same width as the medium box
- cardboard egg box
- spare cardboard sheets
- large dinner plate, about 30 cm/12 inches in diameter
- 9 x paper plates, about 23 cm/9 inches in diameter
- 4 x kitchen roll tubes
- stapler
- orange or red tissue paper
- kitchen foil
- sticky tape
- 5 x toilet roll tubes
- 4 x small foil pie dishes
- 2 x 60-cm/23-inch lengths of wide ribbon
- paints and paintbrushes, crayons and felt-tip pens, to decorate as you wish

Time to make: about 40 minutes

DAD TIP

The suggested size of the large box is around 51 cm/20 inches long x 31 cm/ 12½ inches wide x 31 cm/12½ inches high with the flaps closed. However, the size of box you use is dependent on the size of your child and could be smaller or larger than this. It needs to be rectangular and landscape in shape and big enough to fit over your child with the top edge of the top flaps coming to around waist height.

Step 1:

⚠️ Glue down the flaps on the bottom of the large, rectangular box with a glue gun. Make sure to only apply a line of glue along the short edges of the long flaps, as shown by the blue lines.

Step 2:

Measure with a ruler about 8 cm/3¼ inches in from the short edges of the box and draw a line with a pencil.

⚠️ Use a craft knife and ruler to cut along these two lines making sure you cut through the underlying flaps too.

Step 3:

⚠ Fold the flaps down inside the box and glue them to the sides with a glue gun. This will reinforce the sides a little. Turn the box over.

Step 4:

To make the bonnet of the Monster Truck, draw a diagonal line across one of the long flaps roughly at a 45-degree angle with a ball-point pen and ruler. Push quite hard with the pen to score the surface of the cardboard, making it easier to fold the card. Repeat on the opposite flap.

Step 5:

Lift the flaps up and bend them over.

⚠ Use the glue gun to stick the short flap on top of the two bent flaps to create the slope of the bonnet. Trim off any excess card above the bonnet you've just created from the two long flaps. Draw a line with a pencil and ruler to use as a guide and trim with a craft knife or scissors.

Step 6:

To make the windscreen, open up the smaller cardboard box and lay it out flat. Adjust the size of the template for the windscreen (see page 125) on a photocopier so that the width matches the width of the bonnet of your box.

⚠ Using the template as a guide, draw around it onto the card and cut it out. Glue the long tab to the inside, top edge of the bonnet and the two side tabs to the inside of the box, so that there is a slight slope to the front of the windscreen.

Step 7:

⚠ Cut a couple of squares, measuring about 8 cm/3¼ inches x 8 cm/3¼ inches, from some spare cardboard and fold them in half. Glue one of them to the inside corner of the side and back flap to hold them together. Repeat on the opposite side.

Step 8:

⚠ To make the spoiler, glue together the top flaps only of the open end of the cereal box. Draw a diagonal line across both ends of the cereal box with a pencil and ruler, making sure they are exactly opposite. Cut the box with a craft knife or scissors along one of the diagonal lines and down the length of the box along the crease. Continue to cut along the other diagonal line and finally along the opposite crease of the length of the box. You should now have two identical halves of a box.

Step 9:

⚠ After cutting the box, the end flaps will no longer be held together. Glue the side flaps of one of the box halves so that the angles of the corners of the short sides are slightly greater than 90 degrees. This will hold the spoiler at a slight angle.

Step 10:

⚠ Glue this part to the back of the truck to stand as high as possible above the box. Glue the flaps of the other half of the box together and glue it to sit on top of the spoiler stand that you've just created.

Step 11:

⚠ Cut the lid off the egg box and cut off the highest points from the inside of the lid to make it level. Trim around the edges with scissors to neaten it up, so that you are just left with the six egg cups.

Step 12:

⚠ Glue the egg box to the bonnet of the truck to look like an engine intake.

Step 13:

⚠ To make the wheels, use a dinner plate as a guide to draw a circle about 30 cm/12 inches in diameter, or larger than the paper plates, on some spare cardboard. Cut out the circle with scissors. Glue a paper plate to one side and another to the opposite side of the cardboard circle, making sure they are central. Repeat this another three times. Lay the box on its side and glue two of the wheels to the lower half of the truck, so that they protrude evenly over the front, back and bottom edges of the box. Leave the glue to set and then repeat on the other side, so that the wheels are level.

Step 14:

⚠ To make the exhausts, flatten one end of one of the kitchen roll tubes. Use a stapler to staple the end closed. Repeat with the other three tubes.

Step 15:

⚠ Glue two exhausts to each side of the truck. Add flames by scrunching up the orange tissue paper, adding glue to the end and pushing it down the ends of the tubes.

Step 16:

To make a shiny bumper, measure out a piece of spare cardboard that is 5 cm/2 inches longer than the width of the truck and about 10 cm/ 4 inches wide and then add another 5 cm/2 inches to both ends.

⚠ Cut it out with scissors and crease the card at the 5-cm/2-inch marks. Wrap the card with kitchen foil, securing it with sticky tape.

Step 17:

Draw around two toilet roll tubes onto the back of the bumper.

⚠ Using the circles you've just drawn as a guide, cut two holes a little bigger than the diameter of the toilet roll tubes in the foil only, making sure you don't cut through the card. Glue the two toilet tubes to the bumper in the holes you've just cut from the foil. You may need to cut the length of the tubes down a little if the bumper sits too far off the front of the truck. Repeat steps 16 and 17 for the rear bumper, then glue the bumpers to the front and back of the truck.

Step 18:

⚠ To make the steering wheel, glue a toilet roll tube to the back of a paper plate. Glue the open end of the toilet roll to the inside of the truck at the front.

Step 19:

⚠ Glue two small foil pie dishes to the front of the truck to create lights. Repeat with two more foil pie dishes at the back.

Step 20:

⚠ Glue one end of one of the ribbons to the back of a 5-cm/2-inch x 5-cm/2-inch square of spare corrugated card. Then glue the card to the inside edge of the truck at the front only. Get your child to stand in the truck and hold it so that the wheels are just off the ground. Glue the other end of the ribbon to the inside of the box at the back to create a loop over your child's shoulders. Do the same with the other ribbon. Your child should be able to walk without the wheels scraping on the floor. Decorate the truck as you wish and then it's ready to wear.

DAD TIP

There are lots of areas to glue in this project, which must be done by an adult with a glue gun to hold them securely. Your child can help with the drawing and measuring and they will love decorating the Monster Truck at the end.

Cora The Sock Caterpillar

Make a fun caterpillar out of a sock!

You will need:

- 1 x colourful stripy sock
- toy filling
- knitting yarn
- scissors
- buttons, needles and thread (or felt and glue)

Time to make: about 30 minutes

CREATING THE FIRST SEGMENT

Push a small amount of toy filling down into the toe of the sock. Keep adding more, a little bit at a time, until the foot of the sock is half full. Wrap a piece of yarn around the sock, just behind the stuffing. Pull it tight and tie in a firm knot. You should now have a ball shape at the bottom of the sock.

CREATING THE SECOND SEGMENT

Add more toy filling to the foot of the sock, stopping just before you get to the heel. Tie yarn around the sock to hold the stuffing in place, as before.

CREATING THE THIRD SEGMENT AND THE HEAD

Stuff the heel of the sock and tie in place with yarn, as before, to make a third ball shape. Repeat to make one last segment. This will be the head. You should now have four segments in total, plus an extra piece of sock at the top.

MAKING THE ANTENNAE

⚠ Divide the extra piece of sock in half by making two cuts down towards the head. Stop just before you reach the tied yarn. This leaves you with two flaps.

⚠ Cut one of the flaps into three equal pieces, then stretch each one to make them all slightly longer. Plait the three pieces together (see below), then tie yarn into a bow around the end to secure. (You might need someone to hold the caterpillar for you while you plait.) Repeat with the other flap to create a second antenna.

HOW TO PLAIT

Move the right-hand strip to the left, taking it over the middle strip and pulling it tight. Then, move the left-hand strip to the right, taking it over the middle strip and pulling tight. Repeat, moving the right-hand strip over the middle one again. Keep going, taking it in turns to move the right and left-hand strips over the one in the middle, until you run out of material.

ADDING THE FINISHING TOUCHES

⚠️ To make the eyes, glue two felt circles into place (or sew on some buttons).

DAD TIP

This sock toy is not suitable for children under 3 years of age.

I Am Great!

Make a self-portrait or photo really come to life.

When children draw themselves, they will often create something quite unusual! Fifteen arms, ears for eyes, monkey tails and faces breathing fire — it can be nothing short of bizarre and hilarious. These creations aren't just down to a simple lack of pen control — a large part of it is because most children don't have a very clear sense of self yet and aren't limited by self-consciousness. With that in mind, creating a stunning self-portrait with your child can be an incredibly rewarding activity for both you and them. You will start to explore how your child views themselves and create something that will hopefully last a long time, as well as having a real giggle along the way. And remember, this isn't just going to be a self-portrait; this is an 'I Am Great' portrait...

You will need:

- A4 or larger paper or card
- photo of your child (optional)
- paint
- paintbrushes
- pens, crayons or colouring pencils
- glue
- magazines or photos

For the time capsule:

- plastic container, plastic bag, tape, relevant items, such as a newspaper (see list on page 119).

DRAW YOUR PICTURE

Using whatever medium your child feels happiest with (paint, pens, crayons or colouring pencils), ask your child to draw a picture of themselves in the centre of a large piece of paper or card. The bigger the better really, but A4 or larger will be fine. If your child has a photo of him- or herself that they particularly like, they could use this instead — just print the photo out and stick it in the centre of the paper. Once you've done this first step, you can start to get really creative as you decorate the portrait.

ADD YOUR WORDS

Take out a second piece of paper or card. Get your child to write a brief description of who they are or some phrases that sum them up. This can be anything from between two or three lines to a few paragraphs, depending on your child's age and their love of writing creatively. For younger children, you can write down the description for them as you lead them through a discussion where they talk about themselves. From the self-description, select five to ten words together that capture their feelings about themselves. Paint or write those around the portrait or photo on the other piece of card.

DAD TIP

For a really up-to-date photo, perhaps you could get your child to take a selfie with your phone or tablet and print it off. You could also take a photo of your child holding up today's newspaper if you are planning to use the portrait in a time capsule.

4

DAD TIP

Portraits like these are a great activity to do on a rainy day as they can be created completely inside the home.

GET BUSY WITH THE DECORATION

Gather together some decorative items that you can stick around the portrait to illustrate it. This can include things such as magazine images, photos and drawings, as well as decorative bits and pieces that you find around your house, such as sweet wrappers, stickers or ribbons. Get together anything that will help make the portrait a real reflection of the child and their interests. You can have real fun with this — the goal is for the portrait to be a reflection of all of the different aspects of your child's life. So, if they like music, add musical notes or if they like football, add photos of their favourite team. You can also be slightly more abstract with this. For example, if you have decided your child is brave, you might want to add a picture of a lion or if your child is funny, add some pictures of people laughing.

THE FINISHING TOUCHES

Finally, add your child's name and the date that the portrait was created to the piece of paper or card. Then, to finish off, add 'I Am Great!' to the portrait.

CREATE A TIME CAPSULE

With something so personal, wouldn't it be great to keep this portrait for posterity so you can both look back at it in later years? A good way to preserve this image is to create a time capsule.

To make a time capsule, you will need a large plastic container. Fill the container with your 'I Am Great' portrait, as well as some other items. Here are some suggestions:

- A popular small toy or game from current times (although remind your child they won't get to play with it again for a long time!)
- A newspaper with today's date
- A magazine showing current trends
- Recent photographs of the family
- Some photos of the house and the local neighbourhood
- A ticket stub from a recent cinema, museum or theme-park trip

Wrap the container up in a plastic bag and tape it firmly shut. Either place it somewhere safe and secure inside the house or garage or you could dig a small hole in your garden, just big enough for the capsule to fit into. Make sure you mark the exact spot where you have put the capsule — you could plant your favourite type of plant directly above it so that it will remind you that the time capsule is down there.

DAD TIP

To help and guide your child when making their self-portrait, you could make a self-portrait alongside to show how each step is done.

TEMPLATES

Modelling clay
ball size

Modelling clay
flat size

Wings

Tail

* All templates should
  be photocopied

Fuselage

fold

Classic Glider
page 30

Feet x 2

Nose

Ears x 2

Pom-pom Puppy
page 68

fold

Depth of your box
(see page 107, step 6)

fold

fold

fold

Monster Truck
page 106

Crusher-bot Puppet

page 80

Shadow Puppets
page 100